OPPOSING VIEWPOINTS® SERIES

Offshore Drilling

Margaret Haerens, Book Editor

GREENHAVEN PRESS
A part of Gale, Cengage Learning

HUNTINGTON CITY TOWNSHIP
PUBLIC LIBRARY
255 WEST PARK DRIVE
HUNTINGTON, IN 46750

GALE
CENGAGE Learning

Detroit • New York • San Francisco • New Haven, Conn • Waterville, Maine • London

Christine Nasso, *Publisher*
Elizabeth Des Chenes, *Managing Editor*

© 2010 Greenhaven Press, a part of Gale, Cengage Learning

Gale and Greenhaven Press are registered trademarks used herein under license.

For more information, contact:
Greenhaven Press
27500 Drake Rd.
Farmington Hills, MI 48331-3535
Or you can visit our Internet site at gale.cengage.com

ALL RIGHTS RESERVED.
No part of this work covered by the copyright herein may be reproduced, transmitted, stored, or used in any form or by any means graphic, electronic, or mechanical, including but not limited to photocopying, recording, scanning, digitizing, taping, Web distribution, information networks, or information storage and retrieval systems, except as permitted under Section 107 or 108 of the 1976 United States Copyright Act, without the prior written permission of the publisher.

For product information and technology assistance, contact us at

Gale Customer Support, 1-800-877-4253
For permission to use material from this text or product, submit all requests online at www.cengage.com/permissions

Further permissions questions can be emailed to permissionrequest@cengage.com

Articles in Greenhaven Press anthologies are often edited for length to meet page requirements. In addition, original titles of these works are changed to clearly present the main thesis and to explicitly indicate the author's opinion. Every effort is made to ensure that Greenhaven Press accurately reflects the original intent of the authors. Every effort has been made to trace the owners of copyrighted material.

Cover images © Calum Davidson/Flickr/Getty Images and SambaPhoto/Araquem Alcantara/ Getty Images.

LIBRARY OF CONGRESS CATALOGING-IN-PUBLICATION DATA

Offshore drilling / Margaret Haerens, book editor.
    p. cm. -- (Opposing viewpoints)
    Includes bibliographical references and index.
    ISBN 978-0-7377-4779-9 (hardcover) -- ISBN 978-0-7377-4780-5 (pbk.)
    1. Offshore oil well drilling--Juvenile literature. 2. Critical thinking--Juvenile literature. I. Haerens, Margaret.
    TN871.3.O338 2010
    333.8'232--dc22

                                                                    2009050928

Printed in the United States of America
2 3 4 5 6   15 14 13 12 11

FD181

Offshore Drilling

Other Books of Related Interest:

Opposing Viewpoints Series

Agricultural Subsidies

Cars in America

Endangered Oceans

Global Warming

Current Controversies Series

Carbon Offsets

Conserving the Environment

Global Warming

The Middle East

At Issue Series

Are Natural Disasters Increasing?

The Energy Crisis

Ethanol

Foreign Oil Dependence

"Congress shall make no law . . . abridging the freedom of speech, or of the press."

First Amendment to the U.S. Constitution

The basic foundation of our democracy is the First Amendment guarantee of freedom of expression. The *Opposing Viewpoints* Series is dedicated to the concept of this basic freedom and the idea that it is more important to practice it than to enshrine it.

Contents

Why Consider Opposing Viewpoints?

> *"The only way in which a human being can make some approach to knowing the whole of a subject is by hearing what can be said about it by persons of every variety of opinion and studying all modes in which it can be looked at by every character of mind. No wise man ever acquired his wisdom in any mode but this."*
>
> John Stuart Mill

In our media-intensive culture it is not difficult to find differing opinions. Thousands of newspapers and magazines and dozens of radio and television talk shows resound with differing points of view. The difficulty lies in deciding which opinion to agree with and which "experts" seem the most credible. The more inundated we become with differing opinions and claims, the more essential it is to hone critical reading and thinking skills to evaluate these ideas. Opposing Viewpoints books address this problem directly by presenting stimulating debates that can be used to enhance and teach these skills. The varied opinions contained in each book examine many different aspects of a single issue. While examining these conveniently edited opposing views, readers can develop critical thinking skills such as the ability to compare and contrast authors' credibility, facts, argumentation styles, use of persuasive techniques, and other stylistic tools. In short, the Opposing Viewpoints Series is an ideal way to attain the higher-level thinking and reading skills so essential in a culture of diverse and contradictory opinions.

In addition to providing a tool for critical thinking, Opposing Viewpoints books challenge readers to question their own strongly held opinions and assumptions. Most people form their opinions on the basis of upbringing, peer pressure, and personal, cultural, or professional bias. By reading carefully balanced opposing views, readers must directly confront new ideas as well as the opinions of those with whom they disagree. This is not to argue simplistically that everyone who reads opposing views will—or should—change his or her opinion. Instead, the series enhances readers' understanding of their own views by encouraging confrontation with opposing ideas. Careful examination of others' views can lead to the readers' understanding of the logical inconsistencies in their own opinions, perspective on why they hold an opinion, and the consideration of the possibility that their opinion requires further evaluation.

Evaluating Other Opinions

To ensure that this type of examination occurs, Opposing Viewpoints books present all types of opinions. Prominent spokespeople on different sides of each issue as well as well-known professionals from many disciplines challenge the reader. An additional goal of the series is to provide a forum for other, less known, or even unpopular viewpoints. The opinion of an ordinary person who has had to make the decision to cut off life support from a terminally ill relative, for example, may be just as valuable and provide just as much insight as a medical ethicist's professional opinion. The editors have two additional purposes in including these less known views. One, the editors encourage readers to respect others' opinions—even when not enhanced by professional credibility. It is only by reading or listening to and objectively evaluating others' ideas that one can determine whether they are worthy of consideration. Two, the inclusion of such viewpoints encourages the important critical thinking skill of objectively evaluating an author's credentials and bias. This evaluation will illuminate an author's reasons for taking a particular stance on an issue and will aid in readers' evaluation of the author's ideas.

It is our hope that these books will give readers a deeper understanding of the issues debated and an appreciation of the complexity of even seemingly simple issues when good and honest people disagree. This awareness is particularly important in a democratic society such as ours in which people enter into public debate to determine the common good. Those with whom one disagrees should not be regarded as enemies but rather as people whose views deserve careful examination and may shed light on one's own.

Thomas Jefferson once said that "difference of opinion leads to inquiry, and inquiry to truth." Jefferson, a broadly educated man, argued that "if a nation expects to be ignorant and free . . . it expects what never was and never will be." As individuals and as a nation, it is imperative that we consider the opinions of others and examine them with skill and discernment. The Opposing Viewpoints Series is intended to help readers achieve this goal.

David L. Bender and Bruno Leone,
Founders

Introduction

> "I remain skeptical that new offshore drilling will bring down gas prices in the short term or significantly reduce our oil dependence in the long term, though I do welcome the establishment of a process that will allow us to make future drilling decisions based on science and fact."
>
> *Barack Obama*

On January 28, 1969, an oil drilling platform six miles off the coast of Santa Barbara, California, experienced a blowout after a failed attempt to replace a drill bit. Natural gas, oil, and mud shot up the well and oozed into the ocean, leading to an environmental disaster. Before the well could be capped, 3 million gallons of crude oil gushed into the Pacific Ocean, killing thousands of birds, fish, sea lions, and other marine life. On the ocean's surface, an oil slick measuring eight hundred miles long formed, and ocean tides carried it onto nearly thirty-five miles of scenic California beaches. The local fishing and tourism industries were gutted, as cleanup efforts lasted for months and cost millions of dollars. National news programs broadcast the aftermath of the oil spill, which shocked viewers all over the country not only prompted opposition to any further offshore oil development, but also was thought to have spurred the modern conservation movement. As environmentalist Arent Schuyler contended in a January 28, 1989, interview with the *Los Angeles Times*, "People could see very vividly that their communities could bear the brunt of industrial accidents. They began forming environmental groups to protect their communities and started fighting for legislation to protect the environment."

The Santa Barbara spill proved to be profoundly influential in the national debate over offshore drilling. The spill spurred ocean conservation groups to fight against further offshore exploration and development in a number of areas off the U.S. coastline. Many people who had viewed the devastation to marine life and the pristine beaches along the California coast on television supported these conservation efforts, and politicians took note of public opinion. In 1981, U.S. Congress passed a moratorium on any oil drilling on the Outer Continental Shelf (OCS). The ban covered 85 percent of the country's coastal waters—everywhere except the central and western Gulf of Mexico and some areas off the coast of Alaska. Miles and miles of U.S. beaches and oceans were protected from oil development by American oil companies.

In 2008, however, Congress did not renew the moratorium on new offshore oil exploration and development—in effect opening up nearly 300 million acres off the U.S. coast to oil companies. Many people supported letting the ban end. For example, President George W. Bush was a strong supporter of letting the moratorium run out to allow more offshore oil exploration. In addition, public opinion polls showed that a majority of Americans also supported ending the moratorium.

In the years since the Santa Barbara spill, economic factors have changed. Gas prices have risen sharply. In July 2008, the cost of oil soared to nearly $150 a barrel. At the pumps, American consumers were paying more than $4 for a gallon of gas. The economy also faltered. As unemployment rose, the housing market slumped, and a global financial meltdown threatened America's prosperity. Suddenly the idea of offshore drilling seemed worth the danger of environmental devastation if it meant cheaper gas.

The Bush administration estimated that newly opened coastal areas could yield 18 billion barrels of oil and 76 trillion cubic feet of natural gas, which they argued would lead to cheaper prices at the pumps and a lessened dependence on foreign oil to meet America's energy needs. In turn, money would stay in America instead of going in the pockets of foreign governments opposed to American policies. Supporters of offshore drilling also argued that new technology and advanced production techniques would lessen the chance of environmental disasters.

Critics, however, pointed out that neither the size nor anticipated rate of new domestic production would be sufficient to alter the price of oil on the global market by more than a few cents. Environmentalists and scientists also contested further development, charging that offshore oil wells pose a dangerous threat to the delicate oceanic ecosystem. Although technological progress in offshore oil development and transportation has occurred in the intervening years since the Santa Barbara spill, the chance for a significant spill or accident is still high. For example, the U.S. Minerals Management Service (MMS) reported that in the aftermath of hurricanes Katrina and Rita in 2005, 115 oil platforms and 457 pipelines were destroyed, dumping 741,000 gallons of oil into the Gulf of Mexico. Major spills still have the potential to cause damage on par with or even larger than the Santa Barbara spill.

As the debate between environment and economics played out in newspapers and on television programs all over the country, Ken Salazar assumed leadership of the U.S. Department of the Interior as part of the newly inaugurated Barack Obama administration. Salazar immediately delayed the implementation of the Bush administration's offshore drilling plans, which envisaged energy development from New England to Alaska, including lease sales in areas off California and in the North Atlantic that have been off-limits for a quarter of a century. Although Salazar suggested that some offshore drilling will be allowed, he argued that the Bush plan was too broad in scope. Instead, he proposed a period of further study before oil companies would be allowed to explore and drill for oil and natural gas in the once-protected areas.

The authors of the viewpoints presented in *Opposing Viewpoints: Offshore Drilling* discuss the environmental versus economic debate in the following chapters: Is Offshore Drilling Beneficial for the United States? What Are the Consequences of Offshore Drilling? What Offshore Drilling Policies Should the U.S. Government Consider? and What Other Energy Policies Should the U.S. Government Consider? The information presented in the chapters will provide insight into why offshore drilling has aroused so much controversy and the potential benefits and dangers of further offshore exploration and drilling.

Is Offshore Drilling Beneficial for the United States?

Chapter Preface

Ever since the terrorist attacks of September 11, 2001, the United States has prioritized national security as one of America's most pressing concerns. Endless debates have argued how best to strengthen U.S. national security through measures such as heightened visa and travel restrictions, broadened surveillance activities and capabilities, fortified cybersecurity and financial regulations, and a number of other precautions aimed to protect Americans from domestic or international terrorist attacks. Another key issue in the debate is the country's dependence on foreign oil.

In June 2008, the prominent financial company Morgan Stanley released a statement warning of a "monumental transfer of wealth to oil exporters, which may last beyond our generation, with important geopolitical and security implications." Essentially, Morgan Stanley stated that the United States was taking a big chance with its national security by being so dependent on the import of foreign oil. With oil exporters receiving billions of dollars a day from the sale of oil, this global transfer of money was shifting the global balance of power from the importers to the exporters. Exporters such as Saudi Arabia and Iran are becoming the ones with all the money and power. They have a growing control over the world market and can wreak havoc on U.S. political and economic affairs. Moreover, disruption in oil deliveries because of wars, terrorism, or political reasons would be devastating to the American economy.

Some industry insiders and political commentators view increased offshore drilling for oil and natural gas as a practical way to break the stranglehold foreign oil has on American interests. They believe that by exploiting the potential for offshore drilling, the United States can become more energy independent by importing less foreign oil and thereby limiting the influence the international market has on America. At the very least, it can help the United States transition from foreign oil to alternative sources of energy, such as biofuels or other renewable sources including wind and solar power.

Some experts, however, perceive offshore drilling as an inadequate solution. They argue that the percentage of oil produced through offshore drilling won't make much of a difference in the long run and can result in environmental damage in the meantime. Instead, they push for an immediate investment in developing alternative fuels as the only real solution to alleviating the crippling U.S. dependence on foreign oil. Only by researching and developing clean, accessible forms of energy, these experts argue, can the United States truly strengthen its national security.

The viewpoints collected in the following chapter will investigate the issue of whether offshore drilling is beneficial to the United States. Experts explore whether offshore drilling is environmentally responsible, beneficial for the U.S. economy, and preferable to developing biofuel technology.

> *"'Environmentalists' wake up in the middle of the night sweating and whimpering about offshore oil platforms only because they've never seen what's under them."*

Offshore Drilling Is Environmentally Responsible

Humberto Fontova

Humberto Fontova is an author and a conservative political commentator. In the following viewpoint, he argues that offshore drilling is beneficial for marine life, which flourishes around oil platforms. He says that oil spills that pollute oceans and gulfs mostly occur as a result of oil transportation, not oil drilling.

As you read, consider the following questions:

1. How many barrels of oil does the author estimate can be found off the U.S. coast?

2. According to the author, how many of the roughly thirty-seven hundred platforms in the Gulf of Mexico are located in Louisiana?

Humberto Fontova, "More Offshore Oil Drilling," *FrontPage Magazine*, May 14, 2008. Copyright © 2008 FrontPageMagazine.com. Reproduced by permission of the author.

3. How much more marine life is there around oil production platforms than in the surrounding mud bottoms off the Louisiana Coast, according to a study by Louisiana State University's Sea Grant College Program?

In the early 1960s the law of supply and demand greatly irked Cuba's "Minister of the Economy" Ernesto "Che" Guevara. "No problemo!" he divined one fine morning. I'll simply abolish it by creating a "New Man," with these insufferable Cubans as my guinea pigs. The world's intelligentsia applauded deliriously as 14,000 Cubans were murdered by firing squad, 77,000 drowned or were ripped apart by sharks attempting to flee Guevara's whim, and half a million were herded into political prisons and forced labor camps at bayonet point. All of this out of a Cuban population of 6.5 million meaning that [Fidel] Castro and Che's political incarceration rate topped [Soviet Communist leader Joseph] Stalin's.

And wouldn't you know it? After years of this glorious effort, cheered by everyone from [French philosopher] Jean-Paul Sartre to [liberal Democratic politician] George McGovern and from [writer] Norman Mailer to [documentary filmmaker and political commentator] Michael Moore, that doggone law of supply and demand held firm, while Cuba's per capita income (surpassing half of Europe's in the 1950s) plummeted to nudge Haiti's.

The Myth of Oil Spills

For fear of oil spills, as of 2008, the U.S. federal government and various states ban drilling in thousands upon thousands of square miles off the U.S. coast. These areas, primarily on the Outer Continental Shelf [OCS], hold an estimated 115 billion barrels of oil and 633 trillion cubic feet of natural gas. This leaves America's energy needs increasingly at the mercy of foreign autocrats, despots and maniacs. All the while worldwide demand for oil ratchets ever and ever upward.

At times you'd swear that Che Guevara's bloody lesson (not to mention [Vladimir] Lenin, Mao [Tse-tung], and Pol Pot's) has yet to sink in. Barack Obama, for instance, proposes to solve the problem by slapping a "windfall profits" tax on oil companies. Such "hope" that more federal looting of oil producers will lower prices is not "audacious," it is totally unrealistic.

And that's only part of the idiocy. For those who favor evidence over dogma, a lesson in the "environmental perils" of offshore oil drilling presents itself every bit as starkly, though much less murderously. To wit:

Of the roughly 3,700 offshore oil production platforms in the Gulf of Mexico, roughly 3,200 lie off the Louisiana coast. Yet Louisiana produces one-third of America's commercial fisheries and no major oil spill has ever soiled its coast.

Oil Transportation Is Responsible

On the other hand, Florida, which zealously prohibits from offshore oil drilling, had its gorgeous "Emerald Coast" Panhandle beaches soiled by an ugly oil spill in 1976. This spill, as almost all oil spills, resulted from the transportation of oil—not from the extraction of oil. Assuming dictators such as [Venezuelan president] Hugo Chávez keep selling us oil, we'll need more oil and we'll need to keep transporting it stateside—typically to refineries in Louisiana and Texas.

This path takes those tankers (as the one in 1976) smack in front of Florida's Panhandle beaches. Recall the [Exxon] Valdez, the [Amoco] Cadiz, the Argo Merchant. These were all tanker spills. The production of oil is relatively clean and safe. Again, it's the transportation that presents the greatest risk. And even these spills (though hyped hysterically as environmental catastrophes) always play out as minor blips, those pictures of oil-soaked seagulls notwithstanding. To the horror and anguish of professional greenies, Alaska's Prince William Sound recovered completely. More birds get fried by landing

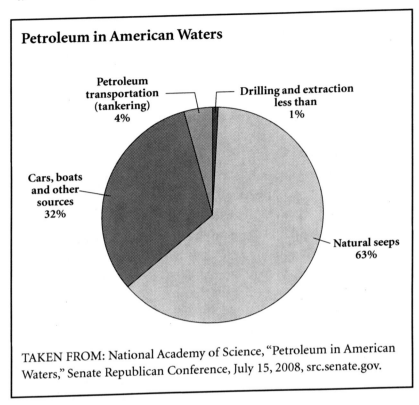

Petroleum in American Waters

Petroleum transportation (tankering) 4%

Drilling and extraction less than 1%

Cars, boats and other sources 32%

Natural seeps 63%

TAKEN FROM: National Academy of Science, "Petroleum in American Waters," Senate Republican Conference, July 15, 2008, src.senate.gov.

on power lines and smashed to pulp against picture windows in one week than perished from three decades of oil spills.

Offshore Drilling Is Good for Marine Life

But forget cheaper oil and less pollution for a second. All fishermen and scuba divers out there should plead with their states to open up offshore oil drilling posthaste. I refer to the fabulous fishing—the EXPLOSION of marine life that accompanies the erection of offshore oil platforms.

"Environmentalists" wake up in the middle of the night sweating and whimpering about offshore oil platforms only because they've never seen what's under them. This proliferation of marine life around the platforms turned on its head every "environmental expert" opinion of its day.

The original plan, mandated by federal environmental "experts" back in the late '40s, was to remove the big, ugly, polluting, environmentally hazardous contraptions as soon as they stopped producing. Fine, said the oil companies.

About 15 years ago, some wells played out off Louisiana and the oil companies tried to comply. Their ears are still ringing from the clamor fishermen put up. Turns out those platforms are going nowhere, and by popular demand of those with a bigger stake in the marine environment than any "environmentalist."

Every "environmental" superstition against these structures was turned on its head. Marine life had EXPLODED around these huge artificial reefs: A study by LSU's [Louisiana State University's] Sea Grant College [Program] shows that 85 percent of Louisiana's fishing trips involve fishing around these platforms. The same study shows that there's 50 times more marine life around an oil production platform than in the surrounding mud bottoms.

An environmental study (by apparently honest scientists) revealed that urban runoff and treated sewage dump 12 times the amount of petroleum into the Gulf than those thousands of oil production platforms. And oil seeping naturally through the ocean floor into the Gulf, where it dissipates over time, accounts for 7 times the amount spilled by rigs and pipelines in any given year.

A Success Story

The Flower Garden Banks coral reefs lie off the Louisiana-Texas border. Unlike any of the Florida Keys reefs, they're surrounded by dozens of offshore oil platforms.

These have been pumping away for the past 50 years. Yet according to G.P. Schmahl, a federal biologist who worked for decades in both places, "The Flower Gardens are much healthier, more pristine than anything in the Florida Keys. It was a surprise to me," he admits. "And I think it's a surprise to most people."

"A key measure of the health of a reef is the amount of area taken up by coral," according to a report by Steve Gittings, the National Oceanic and Atmospheric Administration's [NOAA's] science coordinator for marine sanctuaries. "Louisiana's Flower Garden boasts nearly 50 percent coral cover. In the Florida Keys it can run as little as 5 percent."

Mark Ferrulo, a Florida "environmental activist," uses the very example of Louisiana for his anti–offshore drilling campaign, calling Louisiana's coast "the nation's toilet."

Florida's fishing fleet must love fishing in toilets, and her restaurants serving what's in them. Most of the red snapper you eat in Florida restaurants are caught around Louisiana's oil platforms. We see the Florida-registered boats tied up to them constantly. Sometimes the locals can barely squeeze in.

America desperately needs more domestic oil. In the process of producing it, we'd also get a cheaper tab for broiled red snapper with crabmeat topping.

"When oil spills occur they can bring catastrophic harm to marine life and devastating losses for local businesses."

Offshore Drilling Is Not Environmentally Responsible

Natural Resources Defense Council

The Natural Resources Defense Council (NRDC) works to protect wildlife and wild places and to ensure a healthy environment for all life on Earth. In the following viewpoint, the NRDC contends that offshore drilling poses serious environmental risks including oil spills that can devastate marine life and coastal communities. The NRDC argues that drilling operations are a major cause of pollution and drilling explorations are harmful to a variety of marine life.

As you read, consider the following questions:

1. How long does the NRDC estimate an oil spill in the eastern Gulf of Mexico would take to affect Florida's Panhandle beaches?

2. According to the NRDC, how many oil spills resulted from hurricanes Katrina and Rita?

Natural Resources Defense Council, "Protecting Our Ocean and Coastal Economies: Avoid Unnecessary Risks from Offshore Drilling," February 2009. Copyright © 2009 Natural Resources Defense Council. Reproduced by permission.

3. How many gallons of oil were released into the Gulf of Mexico as a result of these spills?

Healthy oceans are critically important to marine life and to coastal communities whose economies rely on tourism and fishing. Opening up new offshore areas to drilling risks permanent damage to our oceans and beaches without reducing our dependence on oil. When oil spills occur they can bring catastrophic harm to marine life and devastating losses for local businesses. And even routine exploration and drilling activities bring harm to many marine species. The Administration and Congress must work together to assess the environmental impacts of offshore drilling before making key decisions about offshore oil and gas activities in new areas or Alaska.

Offshore Drilling Poses Serious Environmental Risks

Expanded offshore drilling poses the risk of oil spills ruining our beaches from Florida to Maine and along the Pacific Coast, bringing harm to those who live, work, and vacation along the coasts, as well as harming habitats critical to plants and animals.

Oil spills can quickly traverse vast distances. For example, when powered by the Gulf of Mexico's Loop Current, an oil spill in the eastern Gulf of Mexico could affect Florida's Panhandle beaches and even travel around the Florida Keys to wreak havoc on estuaries and beaches from the Everglades to Cape Canaveral. Contamination from the massive 1989 *Exxon Valdez* oil spill [in Alaska] reached shorelines up to 600 miles away; if the spill had occurred on the East Coast, it would have extended from Massachusetts to North Carolina.

In September 2008, Hurricane Ike destroyed oil platforms, tanks, and pipelines throughout the Gulf of Mexico, releasing at least a half-million gallons of crude oil. During hurricanes

Environmental Damage Is Caused by Offshore Oil Exploration and Drilling

Approximately 120 million gallons of oil end up in the world's oceans every year from oil platforms, marine transportation, vessel discharges, and accidents. The impacts of oil on fish and other wildlife are numerous and well known. Ingesting oil is usually lethal, and long-term exposures can result in serious problems, such as reduced reproduction and organ damage.

Each offshore oil platform generates approximately 214,000 pounds of air pollutants a year. These pollutants include precursors to smog, acid rain, and contribute to global warming. Pollution released from rigs can affect people and animals living within 180 miles of that platform.

Ted Danson,
"Environmental and Commercial Perspectives,"
Oversight Hearing before the Committee on Natural Resources,
U.S. House of Representatives, February 11, 2009.

Katrina and Rita there were 125 spills from platforms, rigs, and pipelines on the ocean's Outer Continental Shelf, releasing almost 685,000 gallons of petroleum products. Worse yet, if you include the land-based infrastructure that supports offshore drilling, the damage from these two hurricanes includes 595 spills releasing millions of gallons of oil.

Oil Spills Inflict Devastating Economic Losses Upon Coastal Communities

Oil spills exact a serious toll on coastal economies, including our approximately $35 billion commercial fishing and $60 billion ocean and coastal tourism and recreation industries. The damage and cleanup costs following the *Exxon Valdez* spill were so extensive that Exxon paid out a billion-dollar settlement to the federal and state governments for damages and cleanup costs—and still owes fishermen, Alaska Natives, business owners, and others a billion dollars to redress the spill's harm.

In another example of economic and environmental damage, a July 2008 accident between a chemical tanker and an oil barge discharged more than 270,000 gallons of fuel oil, closing a huge swath of the Lower Mississippi River to vessel traffic for several days. The Port of New Orleans, located at the center of the world's busiest port complex, was shut down and residents were asked to conserve water when water intakes were closed to prevent contamination of drinking water.

Oil Spills Have Lasting Ecological Impacts

According to the National Academy of Sciences, current cleanup methods can only remove a small fraction of the oil spilled into the ocean, leaving the remaining oil to continue affecting ocean ecosystems over time. Scientists investigating the long-term impacts of the *Exxon Valdez* spill estimate that nearly 20,000 gallons of oil from that spill remain in Prince William Sound, continuing to harm threatened and endangered species and undermine their recovery. Marine mammals, sea birds, fish, shellfish, and other sea life are extremely vulnerable to oil pollution and the long-term toxic effects can impair reproductive success for generations. Studies have shown that tiny amounts of oil—as little as one part per billion—can harm pink salmon and cause their eggs to fail.

Spills Aside, Drilling Operations Are a Major Source of Pollution

In addition to environmental damage from oil spills, the routine operations associated with offshore drilling produce many toxic wastes and other forms of pollution. For example, each drill well generates tens of thousands of gallons of waste drilling muds (materials used to lubricate drill bits and maintain pressure) and cuttings. Drilling muds contain toxic metals such as mercury, lead, and cadmium that may bioaccumulate and biomagnify in marine organisms, including in our seafood supply.

The water that is brought up from a given well along with oil and gas, referred to as "produced water," contains its own toxic brew of benzene, arsenic, lead, toluene, and varying amounts of radioactive pollutants. Each oil platform discharges hundreds of thousands of gallons of this produced water daily, contaminating both local waters and those down current from the discharge. An average oil and gas exploration well spews roughly 50 tons of nitrogen oxides, 13 tons of carbon monoxide, 6 tons of sulfur oxides, and 5 tons of volatile organic chemicals.

Drilling Exploration Activities Harm Marine Life

Seismic surveys designed to estimate the size of an oil and gas reserve generate their own environmental problems. To carry out such surveys, ships tow multiple airgun arrays that emit tens of thousands of high-decibel explosive impulses to map the sea floor. The auditory assault from seismic surveys has been found to damage or kill fish eggs and larvae and to impair the hearing and health of fish, making them vulnerable to predators and leaving them unable to locate prey or mates or communicate with each other. These disturbances disrupt and displace important migratory patterns, pushing marine life away fron suitable habitats like nurseries and foraging, mating, spawning, and migratory corridors. In addition, seismic surveys have been implicated in numerous whale beaching and stranding incidents.

Offshore Drilling Results in Onshore Damage

Offshore drilling requires the construction of significant onshore infrastructure such as new roads, pipelines, and processing facilities, which are often built on formerly pristine beaches. Thanks in part to drilling operations, Louisiana is losing roughly 24 square miles of coastal wetlands each year, eating away at natural storm barriers and increasing the risks of storm damage, including damage from oil spills.

Increased Offshore Drilling Will Not Lower the Price of Oil

According to the Department of Energy's Energy Information Administration, drilling in areas previously closed to oil and gas drilling by presidential and congressional actions "would not have a significant impact on domestic crude oil and natural gas production . . . before 2030 (the end of the analysis period)." Even then, "Because oil prices are determined on the international market . . . any impact on average wellhead prices is expected to be insignificant."

Offshore drilling will not lower energy costs, reduce our dependence on foreign oil, or create millions of new jobs the way that investing in clean renewable energy will. Rather than trying to drill our way out of this problem, we must act now to become less dependent on oil and increase our supply of renewable and sustainable energy sources.

"Opening access to America's storehouse of currently locked-up energy resources will not only directly create hundreds of thousands of jobs in the energy-related economy, but save millions more jobs from death by outsourcing."

Offshore Drilling Will Create Jobs and Help the Economy

William F. Jasper

William F. Jasper is known as one of America's top investigative journalists and is senior editor for the New American. *In the following viewpoint, Jasper explains that the United States has resources of oil that could be excavated if offshore drilling on the Outer Continental Shelf (OCS) was permitted. He believes that this offshore drilling not only would produce many jobs and other economic benefits, but also could save many jobs from being outsourced.*

As you read, consider the following questions:

1. According to the U.S. Minerals Management Service, how many barrels of oil does the OCS contain?

William F. Jasper, "Lifeblood from the Ocean Floor: The Lame-Duck Congress Has the Opportunity to Tackle U.S. Dependence on Foreign Oil and Save Hundreds of Billions of Dollars and Millions of Jobs with a Deep-Ocean Drilling Bill," *The New American,* December 11, 2006. Copyright © 2006 American Opinion Publishing Incorporated. Reproduced by permission.

2. According to the article, the DOER Act will have what benefits?

3. What is the high cost of energy causing U.S. companies to do?

Energy dependence has always been an Achilles' heel for Fidel Castro's decrepit Communist regime. From 1959 to 1991, Castro relied on his Soviet sponsors for subsidized oil supplies. More recently, he has been forced to turn to Comrade Hugo Chávez of Venezuela, who has been more than willing to supply his fellow Marxist with discounted oil, to the tune of about 98,000 barrels per day, more than half of Cuba's daily consumption.

But Cuba is set to break out of its decades-old status of energy dependence and economic backwardness. It is sitting on an offshore energy treasure chest that is estimated to contain 4.6 billion barrels of oil and 9.8 trillion cubic feet of natural gas. Over a dozen nations and oil companies have negotiated joint ventures with Havana [the capital of Cuba]—or are in the process of doing so—to cash in on these deep-water energy sources.

So, Cuba, China, Venezuela, Brazil, Canada, India, and others may soon be benefiting from the energy reserves a few miles off our coast. But the United States, which is even more dependent on foreign oil than Cuba, is sitting on the sidelines. Unlike Cuba, which does not have the technical ability to drill for oil and gas on its own, the United States has always been a leader in deep-ocean exploration and drilling. According to the U.S. Minerals Management Service, America's deep seas on the Outer Continental Shelf (OCS) contain 420 trillion cubic feet of natural gas (the U.S. consumes 23 TCF per year) and 86 billion barrels of oil (the U.S. imports 4.5 billion per year). However, federal government policies are preventing us from accessing that treasure trove of desperately needed energy.

No other nation in the world prohibits development of its offshore energy. But, incredibly, federal prohibitions on OCS drilling over the past 25 years have caused the United States to send trillions of dollars to overseas oil producers and have jeopardized our national security by making us dangerously dependent on foreign energy sources. According to the House Resources Committee [officially the Committee on Natural Resources], the United States sends around $500 billion annually to foreign energy producers, which is a major cause of our huge annual trade deficits and the continuing precipitous loss of our manufacturing base.

Getting the Go-Ahead

The lame-duck Congress, which will be back in session for a week before Thanksgiving and then again in early December, has a golden opportunity to do something important that would solve a large part of our energy and trade balance problems. Legislation to open up development of our offshore energy will be on the agenda.

Before the November elections, both houses of Congress passed bills that deal with OCS drilling. The House version, known as the Deep Ocean Energy Resources Act of 2006 (DOER Act, H.R. 4761), is the far more comprehensive of the two, dealing with all U.S. coastal waters. The Senate bill, the Gulf of Mexico Energy Security Act of 2006 (GOMES Act, S. 3711), deals only with a portion of the energy available in the waters along the Gulf states. The House bill, for instance, would open up access to nearly 10 times the reserves of natural gas as the Senate version (86.5 trillion cubic feet versus 9 trillion).

Amazingly, the House's DOER Act passed by a large margin (232 to 187) on June 29, as a bipartisan coalition of labor and business overcame the obstructionist efforts of the radical environmental lobby. "Today marks a historic day for the House of Representatives and the United States," Resources

HUNTINGTON CITY TOWNSHIP
PUBLIC LIBRARY
255 WEST PARK DRIVE
HUNTINGTON, IN 46750

Committee Chairman Richard Pombo (R-Calif.) said, after the
bill passed. "Never before have we accomplished so much for
American jobs and energy security in a single, stand-alone
bill. The DOER Act will finally correct the one-size-fits-all
bans that were enacted during times when energy production
and environmental protection were thought to be mutually
exclusive. They are not, and today a bipartisan majority in the
House voted for both. The balance struck in this bill will save
and create American jobs, lower prices for consumers, and deliver to coastal states unprecedented power to protect 100
miles of their seas."

Bipartisan Bill

The bipartisan majority was obtained in the House by crafting
a bill that intelligently addressed many serious issues and ap-
pealed to many constituencies: industry, union members,
truckers, automobile owners, coastal state governors and legislators, and hurricane-prone communities. The high cost of
energy is making it impossible for many U.S. companies to remain competitive here and is driving them to relocate their
plants overseas.

Plant relocations have been a major factor in the loss of
nearly five million manufacturing jobs in the past 20 years.
Labor union members have been especially hard hit by these
job losses. Opening access to America's storehouse of currently locked-up energy resources will not only directly create
hundreds of thousands of jobs in the energy-related economy,
but save millions more jobs from death by outsourcing.

Another feature of the DOER Act that is responsible for
its bipartisan support is its "states' rights" appeal, which gives
the states control over their own coastal waters while dramatically increasing the revenues available to the states from offshore energy production. Under current policy, states exercise
authority over only waters within three miles of their shores;
the federal government takes over from there out to the 200-

Increase in Annual State and Local Tax Revenues from Production in Previously Unavailable OCS Planning Areas and Additional Refining Capacity

State	Average Increase in Tax Revenues (30 Years)
Alabama	$16,680,387
Alaska	$4,351,540,140
California	$7,492,016,775
Connecticut	$208,798,395
Delaware	$47,396,270
Florida	$2,669,642,414
Georgia	$65,711,876
Illinois	$34,769,027
Louisiana	$260,471,830
Maine	$656,817,596
Maryland	$93,641,613
Massachusetts	$380,302,298
Mississippi	$16,997,939
New Hampshire	$24,127,406
New Jersey	$353,004,224
New York	$325,595,168
North Carolina	$691,716,439
Oregon	$167,655,627
Pennsylvania	$89,114,774
Rhode Island	$143,355,048
South Carolina	$28,043,608
Texas	$175,166,833
Virginia	$269,742,323
Washington	$118,922,838
Total	$18,681,230,849

TAKEN FROM: Joseph R. Mason, "The Economic Contribution of Increased Offshore Oil Exploration and Production to Regional and National Economies," American Energy Alliance, 2009, www.americanenergyalliance.org.

mile limit. Under the DOER Act, states would have complete authority over their coastal waters out to 100 miles.

This turn toward a more sensible federalism would allow individual states to determine for themselves what is best for their people. States under this plan would be free to decide for themselves whether or not to develop their OCS oil and gas reserves, and under what conditions, rather than having these decisions dictated by politicians and bureaucrats in Washington, D.C. The governors of Louisiana, Alabama, Texas, and Mississippi have already spoken on the matter, giving their endorsements to the bill.

With billions of dollars in oil and gas royalties at stake, as well as lower energy prices, it is not difficult to see the reason for high levels of support for the DOER Act among state officials. Louisiana and Mississippi, especially, still reeling from the devastation of Hurricane Katrina, could expect to receive billions of dollars in energy royalties in the years ahead to restore infrastructure destroyed by the storm and protect their people from future catastrophic storm damage. Revenues to both the federal and state governments would also increase from individual and corporate taxes as more oil and gas reserves are drilled and brought online.

In the final days of the 109th Congress, the pressure will be on from the rabid environmental lobby to stop all OCS drilling, while the GOP [Grand Old Party, or Republican] leadership will be pushing for adoption of the Senate's more "moderate" GOMES Act, over the House's DOER Act.

Readers are encouraged to contact their U.S. representatives and senators in support of the House-passed DOER Act, rather than the weaker Senate version.

Offshore, Off-Limits

The current Outer Continental Shelf (OCS) energy dilemma can be traced back to a series of actions begun by Congress in 1982 to stop the federal Department of the Interior from issuing leases for coastal energy development by cutting off appropriations needed to carry out the leasing program. This effectively put 85 percent of the OCS—virtually everything but the western and central Gulf of Mexico—off-limits to development. This lock-up of our desperately needed resources has been a standard feature of the annual Interior Department appropriation ever since.

Not content with this congressional obstruction of our nation's access to energy, the executive branch decided to pile on as well. In 1990, President George Bush (the senior) declared a moratorium prohibiting oil and gas leasing and drilling in "environmentally sensitive areas"—about 99 percent of the California coast, most of Florida's gulf coast, the Georges Bank, and areas off Oregon and Washington—until after the year 2000. In 1998, President Bill Clinton extended the moratorium through 2012. Thus, responsibility for our present predicament can be laid at the feet both of Republicans and Democrats, Congress and the White House.

President Bush and the congressional GOP leadership have made a show over the past six years of trying to open up the Arctic National Wildlife Refuge (ANWR) in Alaska for environmentally safe oil and gas drilling. That has been the president's "number one" energy priority. However, he has never gone to the mat on this issue and used the full weight of his office, as he has done on pushing, for instance, for his federal prescription drug plan or the Central America Free Trade Agreement (CAFTA). Even after the 2004 elections gave him a 55–44 Republican majority in the Senate and $3-a-gallon gasoline gave him strong public support, Bush failed to aggressively push for freeing our ANWR energy resources. Now, in the new Democrat-controlled Congress, opening ANWR is a dead issue.

However, the president could still unilaterally open up some OCS exploration and development by simply canceling the executive moratorium put in place by his father and President Clinton. He has had the power to do that for the past six years, but has not done so. Nor is he likely to do so in his remaining two years. And even if he did remove the moratorium, the next president may reimpose it. Thus the need for the DOER Act, say supporters.

"*Oil and gas development threatens coastlines, harms ecosystems, and directly impacts our tourism, fishing, and real estate economies.*"

Offshore Drilling Will Hurt Tourist and Fishing Industries

Carolyn McCormick

Carolyn McCormick is the managing director of the Outer Banks Visitors Bureau. In the following testimony before the Committee on Natural Resources, she underscores the fact that the U.S. travel and tourism industry and the U.S. fishing industry bring in billions of dollars each year. McCormick contends that the potential risks of offshore oil and natural gas exploration and drilling far outweigh the benefits and that offshore drilling should be opposed to protect the economic revenues coming in every year from coastal industries such as tourism and fishing.

As you read, consider the following questions:

1. According to Carolyn McCormick, the tourism industry employs how many people in North Carolina?

Carolyn McCormick, "Offshore Drilling: Environmental and Commercial Perspectives," Congressional Testimony: Oversight Hearing before the Committee on Natural Resources, February 11, 2009. Reproduced by permission of the author.

2. How many people does McCormick estimate visit the Outer Banks region annually?

3. Tourism is an industry worth how much money, according to the U.S. Travel Association?

Mr. Chairman and members of the Committee [on Natural Resources], again, thank you for this opportunity to be here today. My name is Carolyn McCormick, and I have been serving the public as a tourism and travel director since 1987, beginning in Gary, Indiana, to the state of Indiana, to west Texas, and now to Nags Head, North Carolina, for the last 11 years.

We are here today to help preserve and protect one of America's national treasures, our beaches. We must encourage thoughtful and responsible discourse that recognizes the importance of our coastal tourism centers and our nation's economic needs.

The Tourism Industry

The tourism industry generates trillions of dollars in income and provides memorable experiences to individuals and families worldwide. Tourism brings people and families together outdoors. Working families use the beaches of North Carolina's Outer Banks for vacations with children and their grandchildren and their great-grandchildren. Half of all leisure travelers emphasize the importance of natural settings in deciding their family vacations.

In North Carolina, tourism is a $15.4 billion industry with employment at 184,000 people. The Outer Banks accounts for expenditures of over $1 billion last year [2008] and 20,000 jobs. Dare County's Outer Banks hosts over 5 million visitors from all over the world annually.

The Outer Banks Visitors Bureau's staff and I speak with thousands of visitors and their families every year. In over-

Value of Tourism to Coastal States		
State	Dollars in Billions	Related Jobs
California	93.8	928,700
Florida	62.0	948,700
Georgia	15.4	211,800
Maine	13.6	176,633
Massachusetts	12.5	125,300
New Jersey	37.6	480,800
North Carolina	15.4	187,200
Oregon	7.9	88,900
South Carolina	16.0	208,083
Virginia	16.5	206,900
Total	290.7	3,563,016

Source: NRDC, *Testing the Waters: 2007*, Chapter 2, page 9.
Available at: http://www.nrdc.org/water/oceans/ttw/chap2.pdf

TAKEN FROM: Natural Resources Defense Council, "Protecting Our Ocean and Coastal Economies: Avoid Unnecessary Risks from Offshore Drilling," February 2009, www.nrdc.org.

whelming numbers, they tell us that the natural, cultural and historic resources, primarily the 130-mile stretch of barrier islands along the Outer Banks, are the main reason they visit us. The Outer Banks are truly America's beach, a free and open-access chain of barrier islands off the northeastern coast of North Carolina.

Effects of Offshore Drilling

Oil and gas development threatens coastlines, harms ecosystems, and directly impacts our tourism, fishing, and real estate economies. The people of Dare County have a long and strong history of opposing drilling along the Outer Continental Shelf [OCS]. The towns of Duck, Nags Head, Kill Devil Hills, Kitty Hawk, Southern Shores, Manteo, the County of Dare, and the Dare County Tourism Board have all filed resolutions opposing drilling off the Outer Continental Shelf. The well-documented socioeconomic and environmental risks outweigh the rewards. We need policies that help us cope with climate change on the nation's coastline.

On January 29 [2009], *Winston-Salem Journal* editorial staff put in an op-ed piece. I am going to read a couple of excerpts: "The Interior Department has issued a detailed proposal for oil and gas drilling off both the Pacific and Atlantic Coasts, including the fragile, already-threatened North Carolina coast. Efforts and human ingenuity should concentrate on making the country more energy independent thus seeking alternative fuels that do not, in fact, increase levels of greenhouse gas emissions."

"There's been talk for years about drilling off the North Carolina coast. Many of the state's top leaders have resisted such proposals, fearing that drilling could hurt the tourism this state increasingly depends upon. But when gas prices shot up to record highs last year, some of our elected leaders, like their counterparts nationwide, relaxed their resistance."

"The Interior Department issued its proposal in the last days of the [George W.] Bush administration, which had pushed for more drilling off America's coasts. The draft plan would allow drilling from New England to Florida and off the California coast . . . these areas were recently declared off-limits by Congress. Ken Salazar, the new secretary of the U.S. Department of the Interior, indicated to the Associated Press that he likely would be receptive to scaling back his department's proposal for more oil drilling."

"Drilling rigs would require nearby refineries and storage facilities and create increased traffic between the rigs and refineries. The rigs would threaten the environment especially, if one was knocked over in a hurricane. With the Outer Banks jutting right out into the path of so many storms, that danger would be very, very real."

Oil Development Is at Odds with Coastal Communities

In January of 2009, the state of North Carolina legislative body appointed a group to examine economic and environmental impacts of gas and oil exploration off the coast of North Carolina. That review is expected to be completed in 6 to 8 months.

Again, the industrial character of offshore oil and gas development is often at odds with the existing economic base of the effective coastal communities, many of which rely on tourism, coastal recreation, and fishing. In Dare County, North Carolina, the Outer Banks Visitors Bureau has been fighting efforts to lift the ban on coastal drilling precisely because we realize what a crushing effect coastal drilling could have on our Great Barrier Islands, a $1 billion tourist and fishing economy. If there is one spill, one disaster, the Outer Banks can be impacted for a long time. The powerful hurricanes that battered the Gulf Coast have destroyed drilling platforms, underwater pipelines, and coastal storage tanks, dumping millions of gallons of oil. Drilling in hurricane and storm-plagued waters has proven to be disastrous.

Other Industries Will Be Affected

In addition to potentially catastrophic effects on the tourism industry, drilling for gas and oil off our coast could have significant negative impacts on commercial and recreational fishing, our fisheries, marsh lands, and marine habitat. Jobs and the environment are not mutually exclusive. A balanced economy is based on a clean, healthy marine environment, and efforts need to be focused on restoring our marine environment and sustaining our fisheries.

According to the U.S. Travel Association, tourism in America is a $1.7 trillion industry, with coastal communities representing over $700 billion annually. Last year, travel and tourism generated over $100 billion in tax revenues for state, local, and federal governments. The world tourism industry has identified climate change as key to future strategic planning. United Nations World Tourism Organization [UNWTO] Secretary-General [Francesco] Frangialli, addressing climate change, said, "We," the tourism industry, "are part of the problem," global warming, "and we will be part of the solution."

Social scientists recognize the need to create innovative responses to projected impacts of climate change on tourism. It is incumbent upon all industries, governments, [and] nongovernmental organizations [NGOs] to work together to find solutions to our current energy needs and place a higher emphasis on seeking alternative fuels, wind, reintroducing efficient railway systems, encouraging smarter, more fuel-efficient transport vehicles, while reducing greenhouse gas emissions. We must create real incentives that motivate and drive the ingenuity of all of us to find a cure, not just a treatment that will keep America working, traveling, and living.

> *"The seemingly straightforward answer to the current energy crunch would be to break the stranglehold of the monopoly suppliers by drilling for more oil and natural gas at home."*

Offshore Drilling Will Strengthen Our National Security

Andrew A. Michta

Andrew A. Michta is Professor of National Security Studies at the George C. Marshall European Center for Security Studies in Germany. In the following viewpoint, he suggests that there is a growing realization that energy security and controlling the energy supply is essential to U.S. national security. Michta believes that increasing offshore drilling is therefore imperative to this end.

As you read, consider the following questions:

' 1. What price per barrel of crude oil did Goldman Sachs predict in 2008?

Andrew A. Michta, "Power Failure: The Energy Crunch Emerges as the 21st Century's Top National-Security Issue" *American Conservative*, July 28, 2008. Copyright © 2008 The American Conservative. Reproduced by permission.

2. What is the most common explanation for the energy crunch, according to the author?

3. What other factors does the author identify as affecting the price and supply of oil?

On May 2, 2008, Goldman Sachs finally called it: The super-spike endgame in oil has begun. The price per barrel of crude [oil] could reach $200 in the next six to 24 months, with continued extreme volatility. The report confirmed what the U.S. Department of Energy chooses to ignore but others have been saying since at least 2005: We have entered a period of "peak oil," in which demand consistently outstrips global supply, amid growing uncertainty about the price of energy and the availability of reserves.

About a month later, Morgan Stanley warned of a "monumental transfer of wealth to oil exporters, which may last beyond our generation, with important geopolitical and security implications." Receipts of oil exporters are running as high as several billion dollars per day, with $1 billion going to Saudi Arabia. OPEC's [Organization of the Petroleum Exporting Countries'] surplus this year [2008] is projected to reach $500 billion, with most of it flooding into sovereign wealth funds— essentially investment arms of foreign governments. At the oil price of $135 a barrel, Morgan Stanley estimated that the stock of the proven reserves of the six Gulf Cooperation Council [GCC] countries would be worth about $65 trillion. By comparison, the world's total public equity market capitalization is around $50 trillion.

A glance at the exploding skyline of Dubai [United Arab Emirates (UAE)] tells the story better than reams of market-intelligence reports. We are in the midst of the most massive wealth transfer the world has ever witnessed, and it is driven not by market forces but by an increasingly state-controlled global energy supply monopoly. Unchecked, this economic shift will result in a radical reordering of the global balance of power.

Reasons for Energy Crisis

The most common explanation for the energy crunch is the widening gap between supply and demand, with the culprit—depending on one's ideological predilection—being shady oil companies or skyrocketing consumption in the United States, European Union [EU], China, and India. These explanations are partly true but incomplete.

According to EU projections, between 2002–2030, demand for oil in the United States and Canada will grow by 34 percent from 19.7 million barrels to 26.3 million per day. The EU will see its energy needs expand 15 percent, and Japan and Korea will consume an additional 11 percent. China's demand will grow by a whopping 157 percent over the same period—from 4.9 million barrels per day to 12.7 million—displacing the EU as the second largest consumer of oil. India will consume an additional 124 percent.

But there is little direct connection between present demand and the surge in prices. From 2002 to 2007, the price of oil rose $60 per barrel, then last year it jumped another $60. Consumption, while rising, had scarcely doubled.

Focusing exclusively on market demand assumes that suppliers play by the rules of the marketplace. But in an environment in which resources are nationalized, price is not set by the market. Energy producers' strategic goals and security objectives are driving the supply side of the equation, even as we continue to consider the crisis in pure market terms.

Role of Speculation

Of course, some of the price increase can be associated with speculation, with the flood of new institutional investors or the collapsing dollar. But the most direct explanation points to persistent uncertainty and fear that the emerging oil and gas supplier monopolies—on a scale unseen until now—have the ability to dictate price at will. The relentless escalation is driven by the anticipation that demand will continue to rise while the already limited supply will be kept low by the actions of government-controlled oil and gas cartels, moving toward a complete disconnect between prices and available reserves.

Since the creation of OPEC, the pricing of oil has been an exercise in market manipulation. The openly stated goal of the organization is to control the world oil market by "regulating oil production and production standards." Since its inception, OPEC has shown itself to be one of the most prosperous and effective monopoly alliances in history, notwithstanding occasional cases of individual members acting outside the agreed upon production and pricing targets, as in the mid-1990s when overproduction led to the collapse of the oil price. At the time, the first Gulf War and the dramatic increase in the American military footprint in the Middle East made the United States the guarantor of regional security, in the process creating a strong incentive for Saudi Arabia and Kuwait to keep the spigot wide open. The "roaring nineties" of cheap energy and the soaring stock market followed.

Political Considerations

In the post-9/11 world [after the terrorist attacks of September 11, 2001] the situation has changed dramatically, in part because of the loss of American credibility due to our inability to destroy al Qaeda and the Taliban in Afghanistan and in greater part because of the [George W.] Bush administration's disastrous decision to attack Iraq. The invasion first took the Iraqi oil fields out of play; later, as the country disintegrated into factional fighting, the Iraqis were able to put back online only a portion of their degraded oil capacity. The unintended consequence was the strengthening of Iran's and Saudi Arabia's monopoly position.

The world's largest national oil company, Saudi Aramco, operates more than 9,000 miles of petroleum pipelines throughout Saudi Arabia, including the key 745-mile East-

West Crude Oil Pipeline taken over in 1984 from Mobil and used to transport Arabian Light and Super Light from Abqaiq refineries in the Eastern Province to Red Sea terminals for export to European markets. The Saudi-owned delivery chain extends beyond pipelines and terminals, too: Aramco's shipping subsidiary Vela International Marine has one of the largest fleets of supertankers in the world.

The pattern of maximizing state control over supply is repeated across the region. The National Iranian Oil Company (NIOC) runs all of that country's oil and gas exploration and production. International companies can develop Iranian oil sources only in partnership with an Iranian affiliate. Likewise, state-owned Qatar Petroleum controls each aspect of Qatar's oil sector, including exploration, production, refining, transport, and storage. Kuwait's nationalized oil industry is run by the Kuwait Petroleum Corporation [KPC], with its subsidiary Kuwait Petroleum International managing refining and marketing and the Kuwaiti Oil Tanker Company [KOTC] running shipping. Bahrain Petroleum Company holds similar sway over everything from exploration to distribution, including awarding exploration contracts to international companies. Since 1979, Bahrain's natural gas production has also been nationalized. So too in the United Arab Emirates, which controls 8.5 percent of the global oil supply: The largest state-owned company is the Abu Dhabi National Oil Company [ADNOC], with 17 subsidiary companies in the oil and natural gas sectors. ADNOC has the right to take up to a 60 percent stake in any major oil project. Foreign investors are largely limited to exploration and partnering in building pipeline capacity.

Russia Plays a Factor

Another key development on the road to the cartelization of the global energy supply was the election of Vladimir Putin as Russia's president. Marking the end of the "times of trouble" in Russia, Putin's unwavering goal has been to restore the country's power and international prestige. His strategy was based on an idea that even Russia's most liberal democrats had advocated for years: renationalization of the energy sector to provide steady government revenue. During the Putin presidency and now under Dmitry Medvedev, Russia reconsolidated state control over its energy sector. Through political pressure, hard bargaining, and the selective use of law enforcement—as in the case of jailing Mikhail Khodorkovsky, the owner of Yukos [Oil Company]—Putin and Medvedev have made Russia's energy resources the critical component of the country's national security strategy.

The plan has worked: In 2007, Russia's GDP [gross domestic product] grew by 8.1 percent, marking its seventh consecutive year of growth and surpassing all other G8 [Group of Eight representatives of the world's major industrial nations] members. According to the IMF [International Monetary Fund] and World Bank, Russia's oil and gas sales generated 64 percent of all its export revenue. The government fund set up to manage the windfall was projected in 2007 to be worth $158 billion.

To maximize influence in Europe and the "near abroad," Medvedev will follow Putin's renationalization of Russia's energy with a page from the Arab playbook: the cartelization of natural gas. Russia controls the world's largest supply of natural gas, with nearly twice the reserves of Iran, the second largest producer. In 2007, Gazprom, a de facto national monopoly, controlled 85 percent of all Russian natural gas exports. This year it will invest over $20 billion in natural gas production and transportation.

Creating a Stranglehold on Oil

By expanding its control over gas resources in central Asia through a series of pipeline infrastructure deals, Russia has put itself in a position to negotiate an agreement with Iran to cartelize the global supply of natural gas. Once this happens, the lion's share of oil and gas in the Middle East and Eurasia will be locked into the OPEC/Russia-Iran duopoly. Russia's dominant position in central Asia will also allow Moscow to alleviate pressure on its own energy market and to target liquid natural gas for monopoly control, consolidating its domination of the EU gas market. The resulting revenue—derived from prices set in Moscow and Tehran—may prove much greater in the long run than analysts have been predicting, allowing both Russia and Iran to continue to modernize their militaries.

The security implications are potentially devastating for the United States and the European Union. Russia has natural gas reserves estimated at close to 47.9 trillion cubic feet. Add to that the reserves of central Asia and Iran—Iran holds 24.8 trillion cubic feet—and this new cartel will be able to control the price of natural gas. Russia and Iran are already cooperating over their energy interests. On July 13 [2008], Gazprom signed an agreement with NIOC to help Tehran develop its oil and gas fields. In a meeting with Iran's president Mahmoud Ahmadinejad, Aleksei Miller, CEO of state-controlled Gazprom, pledged his company's commitment to "be a cooperative partner for the Islamic Republic of Iran." The Iranian host reciprocated by calling for "expanding ties with Russia in oil and gas as far as possible." It is also reported that Gazprom will assist in the building of a pipeline to deliver Iranian gas to India and Pakistan. In short, Washington [the president and Congress] should have no illusions that Moscow would risk its relations with Tehran to support America's opposition to an Iranian nuclear program.

20th-Century American Security Policy

American security policy in the 20th century was based on the premise that U.S. global influence could be protected by preserving an open international economic order and by denying any one great power monopoly control over critical areas of

Newt Gingrich on Energy and National Security

While estimates range on the degree to which oil futures trading is affecting the price of oil, there is broad consensus that it is playing a role. The very act of opening America's vast oil deposits for extraction would send an immediate signal to speculators that supply will be increased, and that betting on higher prices for oil is no longer a safe investment. Prices will fall as a result.

Also, beginning the process of drilling for our American oil would allow us the freedom to empty part of the strategic oil reserve into the market on the promise it will be replenished by these future American sources. This immediate increase in the supply of oil would cause a decrease in price.

Newt Gingrich,
"My Message to Democrats: Listen to the People
and Make This 4th of July Energy Independence Day,"
Newt.org, July 1, 2008. www.newt.org.

the world where resources were concentrated. The policy proved sound, as Western Europe, aligned with the United States, quickly recovered from its World War II devastation, while Asia—save Japan—languished, and Russia proved unable to compete with the transatlantic alliance. The policy stabilized Europe and Asia, saw an unprecedented expansion of market democracies, and in the aftermath of the Soviet collapse helped to reconstitute and reunify Europe. The core elements of the U.S. security map—American financial and industrial power in the Western Hemisphere and the technological resources of Europe in Eurasia and Japan in the Pacific—allowed us to act as an offshore balancer in a number of secondary geostrategic regions, including the Middle East. While never a hegemon, the United States was able to balance its commitments and provide security to the key regions of the globe.

Today, the American position and the international security environment are quite different. Formerly the creditor to the world, the United States is now the largest debtor nation, a net importer of capital and energy with a shrinking industrial base. It is engaged in two wars funded through runaway international borrowing. With the accelerated global diffusion of knowledge and technology through internationalized manufacturing, the pivotal points of global stability are to be found in areas that contain the only resource that has not been subject to the competitive pressures of globalization: fuel.

There Is a Risk

The nationalization and cartelization of the global energy supply is returning us to a security paradigm reminiscent of the 19th century, when physical control of resources took precedence over the market. The Middle East, Russia in conjunction with central Asia, parts of Africa, and parts of Latin America are today the four pivots of this new geostrategic energy map.

The inability of the United States and Western Europe to resist the trend toward monopoly control of energy resources—in combination with the more recent failure of both the [Bill] Clinton and Bush administrations to change oil consumption in the United States—has exposed the United States to an unprecedented security risk. By not reacting to the creation of OPEC and allowing the use of the "oil weapon" after the Yom Kippur War [Egypt and Syria attacked Israel in October 1973], Western countries permitted the open energy market to be dismantled.

According to received wisdom, in the new globalized economy, producers and consumers are equally tied to a shared marketplace. But state behavior today strongly suggests that physical control of energy sources trumps all. Today most of the largest reserves, from Saudi Arabia to Mexico to Russia, are run by oil companies that are nationalized or whose majority stock is owned by government. The full spectrum of state power is deployed to ensure maximum control over supply, and economic powerhouses such as China, India, and Russia are adapting to the new geostrategic game. China's neocolonial expansion into Africa is a case in point.

On the U.S. side, there is also a growing realization that control of supply is essential to energy security. The ongoing noncompetitive negotiations between the Iraqi government and ExxonMobil, Shell, Total, and BP to develop and maintain that country's oil fields are presented by the media as defying the nationalizing trend, but they are in line with the actions of other states seeking to secure supply.

Break the Monopoly

The seemingly straightforward answer to the current energy crunch would be to break the stranglehold of the monopoly suppliers by drilling for more oil and natural gas at home. President George W. Bush and Sen. John McCain have recently [in 2008] called for reversing the 27-year ban on offshore drilling. It is estimated that by opening up new drilling on federal land and coasts we could add about 3 million barrels a day to the current U.S. output of some 5.1 million—a significant boost to domestic supply as we develop alternative energy sources.

But we should not delude ourselves that we can drill our way out of the current predicament. Without a commitment from national suppliers in key oil producing states to increase output, as well as major improvements in energy efficiency worldwide, added supply in the United States would not significantly lower the price of oil. More importantly for U.S. national security, oil is only one part of the unfolding global energy squeeze and cannot be treated in isolation.

As reported by the McKinsey Global Institute, pressure is rapidly building in the natural gas and electricity markets as well. Almost three quarters of all natural gas reserves are located in the Middle East and Eurasia: Russia, Iran and Qatar hold 58 percent of global reserves. Back in 2004, the Energy Information Administration projected natural gas consumption worldwide would increase from 100 trillion cubic feet to 163 trillion cubic feet in 2030. More importantly, according to the report, while in 2004 Organisation for Economic Co-operation and Development (OECD) countries accounted for 40 percent of global natural gas production and 52 percent of consumption, in 2030 they will produce 27 percent and consume 43 percent of global output. To put the numbers in perspective, 30 key market democracies will increase natural gas production by only 0.4 percent annually on average, while their consumption will grow at 1.2 percent each year. By 2030, more than one-third of the natural gas consumed by OECD countries will have to be imported.

In the electricity-generation sector, the United States finds itself in an especially difficult situation because of decades of neglect, especially in the area of nuclear power. Since the 1979 Three Mile Island incident [a nuclear power accident in Pennsylvania], building nuclear plants in the United States has been all but politically impossible. Most estimates also find that prospects for expansion of hydroelectric power are limited, as most high-elevation water sources of electricity have already been dammed. And the lead times needed to build coal-fired plants are crippling: Obtaining a new permit for a coal-fired plant in the United States takes five years on average. With the prices of oil and natural gas soaring worldwide, oil- and gas-generated electricity will inevitably lead to higher electricity prices, further undermining the competitive position of U.S. industry.

Danger Is Growing

Today the triple pressure of foreign government-controlled access to oil, the skyrocketing price of natural gas, and the insufficient power-generation sector makes energy the central national security issue for the United States. And the deteriorating situation in the Middle East only compounds stress on the already precarious supply chain. Those anxious about the current combination of high demand and limited supply should consider the impact of a wider war in the Middle East. With oil soaring toward $300 a barrel, there would be no security issue on the horizon other than energy.

In the new security environment, the United States has a choice: continue on the current path of energy dependence in a non-market-driven pricing environment—with ever greater balance of payment problems deindustrialization, transfer of national wealth to the oil producers, and gradual loss of sovereignty—or push with all available government and industry resources to move away from fossil fuels.

After four decades of arguments that globalization has all but obliterated traditional realist concerns about resources, we are about to learn again that there is no substitute for controlling your energy supply. For the United States, an energy policy that makes us independent of foreign energy sources should be our most critical national security goal. We simply cannot continue to transfer hundreds of billions of dollars every year to buy a commodity whose price is arbitrarily set by foreign governments, and in the process bleed the national wealth it took America two centuries to accumulate.

"There is no realistic hope of substantially increasing the supply of oil—drilling in offshore US waters, as favored by President [George W.] Bush and Senator John McCain, will not reverse the long-term decline in US production—so it is only by reducing demand that fundamental market forces can be addressed."

Developing Alternative Fuels Will Strengthen Our National Security

Michael T. Klare

Michael T. Klare is a defense correspondent for the Nation *and a professor of peace and world security studies at Hampshire College. His latest book is titled* Rising Powers, Shrinking Planet: The New Geopolitics of Energy. *In the following viewpoint, he argues that reliance on offshore drilling is not a path to strengthening U.S. national security. Klare states that lessening our dependence on oil through conservation and developing alternative fuels are the only logical answers to the U.S. energy problem.*

Michael T. Klare, "Anatomy of a Price Surge," *The Nation*, June 19, 2008. Copyright © 2008 by The Nation Magazine/The Nation Company, Inc. Reproduced by permission.

As you read, consider the following questions:

1. What does the author believe is to blame for exploding gas prices?

2. How did Vice President Dick Cheney influence U.S. energy policy, according to the author?

3. How does the author view the connection between the George W. Bush administration threats to Iran and oil prices?

As the pain induced by higher oil prices spreads to an ever growing share of the American (and world) population, pundits and politicians have been quick to blame assorted villains—greedy oil companies, heartless commodity speculators and OPEC [Organization of the Petroleum Exporting Countries]. It's true that each of these parties has contributed to and benefited from the steep run-up. But the sharp growth in petroleum costs is due far more to a combination of soaring international demand and slackening supply—compounded by the ruinous policies of the [George W.] Bush administration—than to the behavior of those other actors.

Most, if not all, the damage was avoidable. Shortly after taking office, George W. Bush undertook a sweeping review of US energy policy aimed at expanding the nation's supply of vital fuels. The "reality is the nation has got a real problem when it comes to energy," he declared on March 14, 2001. "We need more sources of energy." At that time many of the problems evident today were already visible. Energy demand in mature industrial nations was continuing to grow as the rising economic dynamos of Asia, especially China, were beginning to make an impact. By 2002 the Department of Energy was predicting that China would soon overtake Japan, becoming the world's second-largest petroleum consumer, and that developing Asia as a whole would account for about one-fourth of global consumption by 2020. Also evident was an unmistakable slowdown in the growth of world production, the telltale sign of an imminent "peaking" in global output.

Bush Administration's Response to Problem

With these trends in mind, many energy experts urged the White House to minimize future reliance on oil, emphasize conservation and rapidly develop climate-friendly alternatives, especially renewables like wind, solar, geothermal and biofuels. But [Vice President] Dick Cheney, who was overseeing the energy review, would have none of this. "Conservation may be a sign of personal virtue," the vice president famously declared in April 2001, "but it is not a sufficient basis ... for sound, comprehensive energy policy." After three months of huddling in secret with top executives of leading US energy companies, he released a plan on May 17 [2001] that, in effect, called for preserving the existing energy system, with its heavy reliance on oil, coal and natural gas.

Because continued reliance on oil would mean increased reliance on imported petroleum, especially from the Middle East, Bush sought to deflect public concern by calling for drilling in the Arctic National Wildlife Refuge [ANWR] and other protected areas. As a result, most public discourse on the Bush/Cheney plan focused on drilling in ANWR, and no attention was paid to the implications of increased dependence on imported oil—even though oil from ANWR, in the most optimistic scenario, would reduce US need for imports (now about 60 percent) by just 4 percent.

But this produced another dilemma for Bush: Increased reliance on imports meant increased vulnerability to disruptions in delivery due to wars and political upheavals. To address this danger, the administration began planning for stepped-up military involvement in major overseas oil zones, especially the Persian Gulf. This was evident, for example, when then Defense Secretary Donald Rumsfeld gave early priority to enhancement of American "power projection" to areas of instability in the developing world. Then came 9/11 [the terrorist attacks of September 11, 2001] and the "war on terror"—giving the White House a perfect opportunity to accelerate the military expansion and to pursue other key objectives. High on the list was the elimination of [Iraqi president] Saddam Hussein, long considered the most potent challenger to US domination of the Gulf and its critical energy supplies.

Real Consequences of Iraq War

But the invasion of Iraq—intended to ensure US control of the Gulf and a stable environment for the expanded production and export of its oil—has had exactly the opposite effect. Despite the many billions spent on oil infrastructure protection and the thousands of lives lost, production in Iraq is no higher today [2008] than it was before the invasion. Iraq has also become a rigorous training ground for extremists throughout the region, some of whom have now migrated to the oil kingdoms of the lower Gulf and begun attacking the facilities there—generating some of the recent spikes in prices.

Then there is the dilemma posed by Iran. With Saddam out of the picture, the Islamic regime in Tehran is viewed in Washington as the greatest threat to US mastery of the Gulf. This threat rests largely on Iran's ability to attack oil shipping in the Gulf and ignite unrest among militant Shiite groups throughout the region, but its apparent pursuit of nuclear weapons has inflated the perceived menace significantly. To restrain Tehran's nuclear ambitions, Washington has imposed economic sanctions on Iran and forced key US allies to abandon plans for developing new oil fields there. As a result Iran, with the world's second-largest reserves after Saudi Arabia, is producing only about half the oil it could—another reason for the global constriction of supply.

US Reaction to Iran

But the administration's greatest contribution to the rising oil prices is its steady stream of threats to attack Iran if it does not back down on the nuclear issue. The Iranians have made it plain that they would retaliate by attempting to block the flow of Gulf oil and otherwise cause turmoil in the energy market. Most analysts assume, therefore, that an encounter will produce a global oil shortage and prices well over $200 per barrel. It is not surprising, then, that every threat by Bush/ Cheney (or their counterparts in Israel) has triggered a sharp rise in prices. This is where speculators enter the picture. Believing that a US-Iranian clash is at least 50 percent likely, some investors are buying futures in oil at $140, $150 or more per barrel, thinking they'll make a killing if there's an attack and prices zoom over $200.

It follows, then, that while the hike in prices is due largely to ever increasing demand chasing insufficiently expanding supply, the Bush administration's energy policies have greatly intensified the problem. By seeking to preserve our oil-based energy system at any cost, and by adding to the "fear factor" in international speculation through its bungled invasion of Iraq and bellicose statements on Iran, it has made a bad problem much worse.

What can be done to reverse this predicament? There is no realistic hope of substantially increasing the supply of oil— drilling in offshore US waters, as favored by President Bush and Senator John McCain, will not reverse the long-term decline in US production—so it is only by reducing demand that fundamental market forces can be addressed. This is best done through a comprehensive program of energy conservation, expanding public transit and accelerating development of energy alternatives. It will take time for some of these efforts to have an impact on prices; others, like reducing speed limits and adding bus routes, would have a more rapid effect. And if this administration truly wanted to spare Americans further pain at the pump, there is one thing it could do that would have an immediate effect: declare that military force is not an acceptable option in the struggle with Iran. Such a declaration would take the wind out of the sails of speculators and set the course for a drop in prices.

> *"Not only has the Democrat Party left us vulnerable to other oil-producing nations, but its ethanol agenda has created vast imbalances in the world's food supplies as corn is diverted from domestic use and as a factor in our agricultural exports."*

Offshore Drilling Is More Beneficial than Biofuels

Alan Caruba

Alan Caruba is a conservative commentator and author. In the following viewpoint, he asserts that the Democrats' advocacy of renewable energy—particularly ethanol—has been disastrous and diverts a more practical and effective solution to the energy problem: more offshore oil drilling. Caruba also argues that clean energy such as solar or wind power is just not a viable solution at this time and points to increased domestic oil drilling.

As you read, consider the following questions:

1. What percentage of the world's oil supply is controlled by monarchical, corrupt, and Communist governments, according to the author?

Alan Caruba, "Democrat Deceptions About Oil," Intellectual Conservative, September 7, 2008. Copyright © 2008 by Alan Caruba. Reproduced by permission of the author.

2. What percentage of U.S. energy needs is fulfilled by clean energy such as wind and solar?

3. What will be the U.S. governmental subsidy of ethanol in 2022, according to the author?

Lost amidst the many speeches delivered at the [2008] Democratic National Convention was one by senator Harry Reid of Nevada. He is the Senate Majority Leader and, as such, controls the legislative agenda in that upper house of Congress. Harry Reid hates oil, but then, so does the Democrat Party.

The reason this nation is held hostage to other oil-producing nations is that the Democrats, going back to president Jimmy Carter, have waged war on the American oil industry. This is especially important insofar as nations ruled by monarchies, corrupt, and Communist governments control 75% of the world's oil.

Democratic Party Sabotaging American Interests

Seldon B. Graham Jr., the author of *Why Your Gasoline Prices Are High*, a petroleum engineer and attorney, recently noted that "it is no secret that Democrats are for renewable energy and are against U.S. oil and drilling for U.S. oil. But, Democrats conceal the fact that they have held this position for three decades. Democrats are not about to change their thirty-year-old energy agenda."

"Thirty years ago, Democrats selected ethanol as their renewable energy of choice. Their ethanol agenda has proven to be a total disaster. But, it is a well-hidden disaster. Democrats continue to push ethanol as the renewable biofuel which will eliminate our dependence on foreign oil and our necessity to drill for U.S. oil. It is surprising that Democrats have been able to fool so many Americans about ethanol for so long."

Not only has the Democrat Party left us vulnerable to other oil-producing nations, but its ethanol agenda has created vast imbalances in the world's food supplies as corn is diverted from domestic use and as a factor in our agricultural exports.

If you had heard Senator Reid, a man who has said, "Oil makes us sick. Coal makes us sick. Global warming makes us sick," you would have heard him attack oil as the reason for all the woes of the world. "President Carter warned us about it in the 1970s when he proposed real solutions—conservation, fuel efficiency, and alternative fuels—to what he correctly named the 'moral equivalent of war.'" President Carter, whose weak response to the taking of U.S. diplomats hostage by the Iranian Revolution led to the election of Ronald Reagan, was wrong then and he is wrong now.

Truth About Ethanol

So-called "clean energy," wind and solar, provides barely one percent of the nation's need for electrical power. It does so only because of the massive subsidies, like those for ethanol, the federal government provides, but Harry Reid could not resist characterizing the Bush administration as rife with "oil industry cronies."

He made no reference, however, to the Democrats' agriculture cronies. As Graham points out, "Democrats gave ethanol a 40¢ per gallon government subsidy in 1978. In 1980, Democrats gave insured loans to build ethanol plants."

"Currently, the government subsidy is 51¢ per gallon through 2010. Last year [2007], the government subsidy payout for ethanol was $3.3 billion. The government subsidy will increase to $18.4 billion in 2022. Ethanol is causing severe economic harm to the American economy, not even considering the increase in the cost of all food products made from corn."

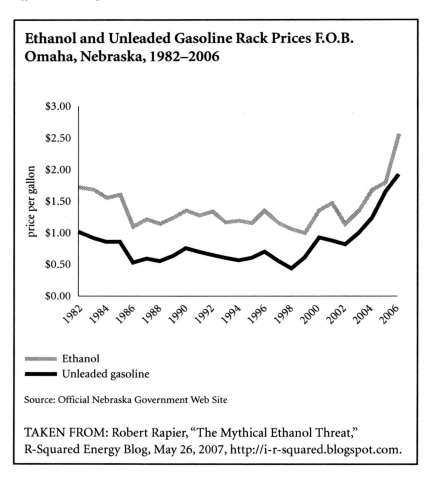

Ethanol and Unleaded Gasoline Rack Prices F.O.B. Omaha, Nebraska, 1982–2006

Ethanol

Unleaded gasoline

Source: Official Nebraska Government Web Site

TAKEN FROM: Robert Rapier, "The Mythical Ethanol Threat," R-Squared Energy Blog, May 26, 2007, http://i-r-squared.blogspot.com.

This is occurring as Americans struggle to find the money to fill their gas tanks and many worry about the price of oil to heat their homes this winter.

Senator Reid praised the Democrat candidate for president, Barack Obama, saying, "He articulates a vision of energy independence that is comprehensive and based on sound science and sound policies. . . ." This is a lie. No nation on earth can be or is energy independent. Even Iran has to import gasoline because it lacks the refining capacity to provide it despite its own vast oil reserves.

United States Needs Oil Refineries

America, too, needs more refineries, but the threat of "wind-fall profits" taxes has kept our oil industry from making the vast, billion-dollar investments necessary to build them and a matrix of environmental regulations has made it even more costly and difficult.

The Democrats and their choice for the next president have resisted permitting our own oil companies to drill for millions of barrels of known oil reserves in Alaska's ANWR [Arctic National Wildlife Refuge] and have resisted lifting restrictions on exploration and extraction of oil on 85% of our nation's continental shelf.

Instead Senator Reid called for more wind power, geothermal, and solar power generation. He called for "smarter vehicles, more efficient and accessible mass transit, energy-efficient building codes. . . ." These are the illusions the Democrats offer in contrast to realistic, pragmatic and vitally needed responses to our need for increased oil and natural gas production.

The Democrats offer the lie that such production would not impact the current price of oil or our needs for "ten years." The mere mention of offshore production caused the price of oil to drop when offered by Senator [John] McCain. The end of the ethanol debacle would lower the price of gas at the pump. Drill now. Drill here. That's the answer.

> *"Because we could grow, harvest, and produce algae-based green fuels here in the US, there would be no expensive and polluting transportation from the Middle East, and no energy-intensive drilling or prospecting."*

Developing Biofuels Is More Beneficial than Offshore Drilling

Chris Dannen

Chris Dannen is a correspondent for Discover *magazine. In the following viewpoint, Dannen is excited about the development prospects of "green diesel," or an alternative fuel derived from algae. Dannen notes that such new, more efficient biofuels are preferable to relying on foreign oil or domestic drilling.*

As you read, consider the following questions:

1. Alternative fuels derived from sugar or corn have driven up the price of food worldwide by how much, according to the author?

2. What does the author cite as advantages of green fuel over petroleum or other alternative fuels?

Chris Dannen, "The Second Coming of Biofuels," *Discover Magazine*, September 2, 2008. Copyright 2008 Discover Magazine. Reproduced by permission of the author.

3. According to the author, green fuels production would come with what carbon cost as compared to petroleum-derived fuel?

Somewhere between fifth and sixth gear in this roaring, turbo-charged Audi A5, I realize I'm not that excited about electric cars.

As an eco-conscious citizen, I should be a little ashamed of my attachment to pistons and gears. But in this test drive, I don't have to be. While the Audi I'm test-driving is a regular production car, the fuel inside it is a new, ultra-potent kind of biofuel that has only a quarter of the per-gallon carbon footprint of petroleum-derived fuel. Sure, that doesn't sound that exciting compared to a zero-emission electric car—until you consider that this new fuel doesn't require new car factories, new fueling infrastructure, or the turnover of our existing fleet of vehicles, all of which are expensive, massively polluting ventures. Could it be that the greenest car on the market is already in your garage—it just needs a new kind of juice?

The New Plant Fuel

"Green diesel," as it's being called, isn't the first effort to use plants to power cars; your gas tank probably has a blend of gas and plant-derived ethanol inside it right now. But it's hard to get excited about biofuels when they already have such a bad rep. The use of corn and sugar in fuels has driven up the cost of food by a whopping 75 percent worldwide, according to a recent report by the World Bank. And a Nobel Prize–winning chemist has publicized his findings that biofuels made from nitrogen-thirsty plants (like corn and canola) actually produce a net *increase* in greenhouse gas emissions, because they release nitrous oxide during their production. As if all that wasn't bad enough, ethanol blends hurt your car's fuel economy. Not exactly the makings of a green energy panacea.

But high-performance green diesel and gas aren't like other biofuels; they're perfect substitutes for petroleum-derived fuels, except they're made from plant matter like forest detritus, also known as cellulosic waste, or from algae. Green fuels can also be refined on the exact same equipment that refines petroleum. By contrast, traditional ethanol requires new equipment and uses edible plants like corn and sugar that need rich farmland to grow.

Also unlike traditional ethanol, green fuels can also be used in gas tanks in 100 percent concentrations; their cetane numbers, or combustion quality, are actually higher than those of petroleum fuel. That means they could also be used to power jet airplanes, another prime polluter. To boot, green fuels are also more stable and have a lower cloud point than other biofuels. Regular ethanol breaks down over time when it sits in your tank, and turns viscous and sludgy in cold weather.

The secret to this high-performance green stuff is in the production. The refinement of green diesel uses a process called catalytic hydroprocessing. Put simply, cellulosic oils and greases are fed into a "diesel hydrotreater" with a small amount of petrodiesel, and hydrogen is forced into the mixture. That starts a catalytic reaction, the product of which is a potent petroleum substitute. What differentiates this process from traditional biofuel production is the infusion of hydrogen—it removes the dilutive oxygen that most biofuels contain, leaving only the combustible isoparaffins and paraffins, which are indistinguishable from the molecules in refined petroleum. The only by-product of the process is propane, which can be reintroduced into the production loop as a source of hydrogen.

But Will It Scale?

When you crunch the numbers, the implications of using the most advanced of these feedstocks, algae oil, are tremendous. Replacing just 20 percent of America's current thirst for gasoline with current biofuels made from conventional feedstocks like soy or sugar would require a mass of farmland the size of California, Indiana, Nevada and Michigan combined—260

Future of Biofuels

The future of sustainable biofuels may lie with the cellulose derived from various plants. (That's the part of the plant you don't eat.) High oil prices, federal and state incentives, and the drawbacks associated with today's biofuels have all spurred researchers to develop cellulosic fuels.

Once commercialized, these new biofuels can be adopted far more widely—and we'll be able to produce fuel [that] doesn't compete with food for land. Fast-growing, cost-efficient trees, such as poplar and eucalyptus, and grasses such as switchgrass and alfalfa could all be harvested as cellulosic biofuels.

Natural Resources Defense Council,
"Homegrown Energy from Biofuels," 2009.
www.nrdc.org.

million acres—devoted only to growing fuel. That's because plants like soy make for a terribly low oil yield: about 100 gallons of oil per acre. Compare that to algae, which can generate 3,500 gallons of oil per acre, and green diesel starts looking feasible on a large scale. Plus, algae can grow well in arid land, so it wouldn't take up valuable farmland in the Midwest. Build a shallow, algae-growing pool of salt water about the size of Rhode Island under the hot New Mexico sun and you could replace that same 20 percent of our gasoline demand. The saline pools wouldn't use up potable water and could perhaps double as cooling channels for nuclear power plants.

Then there are the fringe benefits: Because we could grow, harvest, and produce algae-based green fuels here in the US, there would be no expensive and polluting transportation from the Middle East, and no energy-intensive drilling or prospecting. That would mean production could come with a 75 percent smaller carbon cost as compared to petro-fuel—not to mention reduced reliance on OPEC [Organization of the Petroleum Exporting Countries]. Suddenly biofuels are looking like a hot prospect again.

A Solution in Motion

No matter how fast and guilt-free this Audi feels, revolutions aren't guaranteed and they don't happen overnight: A lot of the technology that is required to scale up the production of green fuel is still in development, and green fuels in general need statutory mandates to attain popular use. Oil is becoming increasingly difficult to find and extract, but it's still much more profitable than developing alternate fuels. Strong legislation and tax incentives are necessary to encourage investment in biofuels if they are to be produced widely and efficiently.

But there's some big money behind green fuel so far: UOP, a division of energy company Honeywell, is one company researching the new fuel. It's one of the world's largest petroleum research companies, with its technologies at work in the production of over 60 percent of the world's gasoline. Even though it's currently entrenched in the oil industry—it's one of the world's largest petroleum research companies—UOP created a renewable energy unit dedicated to green fuels in 2006.

UOP has already licensed green diesel technology to two European refiners, one of which, Eni S.p.A., intends to have a plant operational in Livorno, Italy, by 2009. It is UOP's research and development folks who've lent me the Audi full of green diesel in the hopes of demonstrating that it is indeed possible to make a biofuel that results in lower emissions, lower carbon footprint, and lower cost—all while behaving like a wild explosive inside your engine.

According to UOP's time line, refiners will start out using conventional vegetable oils as raw materials, called "feedstocks" in fuel jargon. Within three to five years, they hope to move to more sustainable and efficient feedstocks like forest waste, crop residuals, and municipal solid waste before transitioning finally to inedible plant oils like camelina, jatropha, and algae oil. As the collection methods for these feedstocks improve, production will grow.

The production process of green diesel was developed ahead of green gasoline—which would be more useful in the US—but UOP is presently in licensing talks with several unnamed North American refiners, too.

Other big names like BP and ConocoPhillips are also investing in the conversion of cellulosic material to fuel, and venture capital firms are lining up to put money into research and development, according to Daniel Sperling, director of the Institute of Transportation Studies at the University of California, Davis, and the coauthor of a forthcoming book about the future of fuels, cars, and energy policy. Sperling says Congress's most recent biofuels mandate requires 36 billion gallons of nonpetroleum fuel to be in our gas tanks by 2022, 15 billion gallons of which must be advanced, non-ethanol biofuels like green diesel.

Not so Fast...

Despite the high hopes, there are still factors that could bring down biofuel's resurgence. "Algae looks promising, but the volumes of fuel we'd need to produce are just huge," says Sperling. "None of these fuels are obvious winners yet, on a large scale. They'll all certainly be produced in the future, but it's unclear just how successful they'll be." That's thanks to a laundry list of variables that could vitiate their progress: hitches in the collection of cellulosic material, trouble converting land to agricultural development, or ineffectual government support.

Dr. Jennifer Holmgren is the director of UOP's renewable energy and chemicals division. While she's optimistic about the benefits of their green fuel technology, she concedes that our national energy demand is growing faster than any one solution. "I don't believe in a future without petroleum, honestly," she says. "The demand for fuel is just growing too fast. I think we'll need to make a transition to a point where our fuel is coming from other feedstocks in *combination* with petroleum." That means that despite the promise of biomass as a petroleum substitute, demand will require not simply petrofuel or biofuel or electric cars, but *all three.*

So with green fuel on the three-to-five-year horizon, what will our transportation energy look like in a decade? "It will depend on where you live," says Sperling. Midwesterners, for example, might use more cellulosic waste-based green fuel because of their abundance of farm land, while Southwesterners use algae-based green fuel. People in Texas will plug in electric vehicles [EVs] to their wind-powered grid, while Northeasterners might rely on nuclear-generated electricity. A multifaceted solution isn't as exciting as a silver bullet concept car, but luckily it doesn't have to be—it just needs to work.

At present, however, the stars seem to be aligning for green fuel, even if consumers are busy drooling over newfangled hybrids and EVs.

Periodical Bibliography

The following articles have been selected to supplement the diverse views presented in this chapter.

Robert Bryce   "The Democrats and Off-Shore Drilling,"
                      CounterPunch, July 2, 2008.

Robert Bryce   "Why the Promise of Biofuels Is a Lie,"
                      CounterPunch, February 19, 2009.

Alan Farago   "The Off-Shore Drilling Scam," *CounterPunch*,
                      June 21, 2008.

Charles Krauthammer   "On Energy, Do Everything," *National Review
                      Online*, August 8, 2008. www.nationalreview
                      .com.

Andrew Leonard   "Gas Prices and Offshore Drilling," Salon.com,
                      June 18, 2008. www.salon.com.

Deroy Murdock   "Offshore Drilling: Cleaner than Mother Na-
                      ture," *National Review Online*, July 28, 2008.
                      www.nationalreview.com.

Robert J. Samuelson   "The Bias Against Oil and Gas," *Newsweek*,
                      May 18, 2009.

William Tucker   "Biofuels Meltdown," *American Spectator*,
                      February 13, 2008.

Jon Basil Utley   "Obama and the Alternative Energy Fiasco,"
                      Reason, May 13, 2009.

Bryan Walsh   "Putting US Energy in the Wrong Place,"
                      TIME, August 20, 2008.

Bryan Walsh   "The Trouble with Biofuels," *TIME*, February
                      14, 2008.

CHAPTER 2

What Are the Consequences of Offshore Drilling?

Chapter Preface

After crude oil reached a low price of $16 per barrel in 1999, consumers were shocked when crude oil prices went through the roof in the first few years of the twenty-first century. In 2005, prices per barrel reached $65; a year later, they were up to $77. By July 2008, prices had skyrocketed to $145 per barrel. These rising prices were reflected at the pumps. The American economy was starting to slump and American consumers were forced to pay more and more to fill their gas tanks. Politicians quickly realized that they needed to come up with solutions to alleviate the growing problem. Offshore drilling—once an issue simmering on the back burner of American politics—became a viable and politically controversial solution.

One of the main arguments in favor of domestic offshore oil drilling is that it will immediately lower the prices at the pump for the American consumer. Domestic offshore drilling, some experts argue, will lessen U.S. dependence on foreign imported oil and, therefore, lessen the financial stranglehold the Organization of the Petroleum Exporting Countries (OPEC) has on setting the oil supply and prices per barrel of oil. OPEC, a cartel of thirteen oil-producing and oil-exporting nations located in the Middle East, Africa, and Central and South America, essentially controls the global oil market by controlling the oil supply and setting crude oil prices. Some commentators argue that allowing companies to explore and develop oil reserves on the U.S. Outer Continental Shelf (OCS) can provide some relief for both the American consumer, who has been hit hard by the global economic downturn, and the American economy, which relies on affordable energy to transport goods and services across long distances.

Critics, however, contend that neither the size nor anticipated rate of new domestic production would be sufficient to alter the price of oil on the global market by more than a few cents. In addition, offshore drilling would not insulate consumers from price shocks, since the share of oil used in the U.S. economy would not decrease. They dismiss the claim that offshore drilling will provide the relief that American consumers need in such difficult economic times as a cynical attempt to enrich the oil companies at the expense of consumers and the environment.

The question of whether offshore drilling will result in a substantial decrease in oil prices is debated in the following chapter, which investigates the consequences of domestic offshore drilling. Additional viewpoints explore the issue of energy independence, the relationship between offshore drilling and global warming, and the implications of offshore drilling on the standard of living for the American middle class and multinational oil companies.

| "Offshore drilling would also further the goal of decreasing U.S. reliance on oil from hostile nations without losing the beneficial gains from trade."

Offshore Drilling Will Decrease Our Dependence on Foreign Oil

Arthur B. Laffer

Arthur B. Laffer is the chairman of Laffer Associates and a conservative commentator. In the following viewpoint, he derides the idea of "energy independence" put forth by the Barack Obama administration, saying that it would drive oil prices skyward in the United States and provide cheap oil for our economic rivals, such as China. Instead of just opposing offshore drilling, Laffer argues, the United States should pursue policies to wean us off oil produced by hostile foreign nations.

As you read, consider the following questions:

1. According to the author, how much of the oil that the United States uses is imported from foreign countries?

Arthur B. Laffer, "Obama Should Forget About Energy Independence," *The Wall Street Journal*, December 18, 2008, p. A17, Opinion. © 2008 Dow Jones & Company. All rights reserved. Reprinted with permission of The Wall Street Journal and the author.

2. What does the author believe an energy independent United States would look like?

3. Why is the Barack Obama administration's plan to create jobs in alternative energy hollow, according to Arthur B. Laffer?

This week [December 2008] in Chicago, President-Elect Barack Obama introduced key members of his new energy and environmental team and gave a statement expressing his administration's ambitious goal to make America energy independent. While his desire to do so is sincere, such a strategy would be disastrous for our economy.

The platitude of "energy independence" makes zero economic sense. Yes, it's true that many nations that supply us with oil are run by anti-American governments. But unfortunately embargoes don't overturn despotic regimes. More often than not they harden them, as in Zimbabwe, North Korea and Cuba. Since the United States is so reliant on oil, embargoes will hurt the United States as much, if not more, than the countries of OPEC [Organization of the Petroleum Exporting Countries]. The issue of how to handle the anti-American nature of oil-exporting nations is not for the Department of Commerce, but for the White House, the State Department and perhaps the Department of Defense.

Energy Independence Is a Farce

The United States currently imports some 60% of the oil we use. To imagine an energy-independent United States today is to envision gas at $20 or more per gallon and a true depression. President Dwight D. Eisenhower tried oil import tariffs in the 1950s, as has every president since. Yet never before has America's reliance on foreign oil been greater than it is now.

While energy independence for the United States would enormously increase the price of oil at home, it would have the exact opposite effect in the rest of the world. Cheap oil for

Technically Recoverable Undiscovered Oil and Natural Gas Resources in the Lower 48 Outer Continental Shelf as of January 1, 2003

OCS areas	Crude oil (billion barrels)	Natural gas (trillion cubic feet)
Available for leasing and development		
Eastern Gulf of Mexico	2.27	10.14
Central Gulf of Mexico	22.67	113.61
Western Gulf of Mexico	15.98	86.62
Total available	**40.92**	**210.37**
Unavailable for leasing and development		
Washington-Oregon	0.40	2.28
Northern California	2.08	3.58
Central California	2.31	2.41
Southern California	5.58	9.75
Eastern Gulf of Mexico	3.98	22.16
Atlantic	3.82	36.99
Total unavailable	**18.17**	**77.17**
Total Lower 48 OCS	**59.09**	**287.54**

TAKEN FROM: "Offshore Drilling: A Few Useful Facts," *The Oil Drum,* June 18, 2008, www.theoildrum.com.

countries like China would surely not benefit the United States or the world's environment. Businesses that use oil would move offshore, costing American jobs while still polluting the world's environment. Artificial energy independence is neither a good foreign policy nor a good domestic economic policy.

Better U.S. Drilling

Mr. Obama's team is also prejudiced against offshore drilling and nuclear power. Goodness knows no one wants oil splattered all over our beaches, but if we don't drill offshore, Indonesia will. Surely our safeguards are better than Indonesia's. Any trade-off of Indonesian offshore drilling with U.S. offshore drilling is a no-brainer. Offshore drilling would also further the goal of decreasing U.S. reliance on oil from hostile nations without losing the beneficial gains from trade.

Pursuing nuclear power is another important option if we aim to reduce our carbon footprint and reliance on oil from hostile nations. Currently the United States is way behind the curve. Given the vast proliferation of nuclear power worldwide, its cleanliness, its efficiency, and its low cost, surely nuclear should not be "off the table" as the Obama team contends.

The Obama team's chatter about creating jobs in alternative renewable energies is hollow to say the least. Here's why: Any serious attempt to reduce carbon emissions must ultimately rely on a very large tax on the use of fossil fuels. And a very large tax on fossil fuels as an add-on to the taxes we already pay would drive the economy deeper into the ground—with or without alternative renewable energy jobs.

Reasonable Policies

The only real solution is [environmental activist and former vice president] Al Gore's proposal to offset a carbon tax dollar-for-dollar with either an income or payroll tax reduction. If a carbon tax increase were offset dollar-for-dollar with an income tax rate cut, I for one would strongly support the policy. The economy would benefit because the progressive income tax does far more damage than a carbon tax would, and we'd use less oil. It's a win-win situation. Yet this perspective appears to be totally outside the Obama team's ken.

It's telling that Mr. Obama and his appointees kept pointing to the successes achieved by California as examples of what should be done on a national level. Whenever California's current policies—full of taxes and regulations that are crippling its economy—are held up as a model, you know the speaker has a lot to learn.

> *"The notion that Americans can achieve energy independence by drilling off-shore wells and in the Arctic is absurd."*

Offshore Drilling Will Not Lead to Energy Independence

Paul Craig Roberts

Paul Craig Roberts was assistant secretary of the U.S Depart-ment of the Treasury in the Ronald Reagan administration. He was associate editor of the Wall Street Journal *editorial page and contributing editor of the* National Review. *In the following viewpoint, Roberts rejects arguments that offshore drilling would lead to energy independence and bring down the cost of oil. Rob-erts asserts that offshore oil would make a negligible effect on America's dependence on foreign oil, especially in the short term.*

As you read, consider the following questions:

1. What does the author believe that Republicans mean by "energy independence"?

2. In what year would oil produced by offshore drilling become available, according to the author?

3. Bringing offshore oil into production would increase total U.S. oil production by how much?

Paul Craig Roberts, "The Moronic Party," *CounterPunch*, August 11, 2008. Copyright © 2008 CounterPunch, LLP. Reproduced by permission. www.counterpunch.org.

"Although it is not true that all conservatives are stupid people, it is true that most stupid people are conservative."

—*John Stuart Mill*

M any years ago, during the 1970s if memory serves, neo-conservative Irving Kristol, echoing John Stuart Mill, called his conservative party, the Republican Party, "the stupid party."

Kristol was referring to the Republicans' inability to compete on the policy front. Jack Kemp and Ronald Reagan led the Republicans out of the wilderness, but now Republicans have reverted to the stupid party, or more precisely the moronic party.

The "Stupid" Party

Take a minute to examine the presidential campaign propaganda that Republicans send around the Internet, and you will see what I mean. For example, recently while [Democratic presidential candidate Barack] Obama was traveling abroad, showing himself to the remnant of our allies, Republican political operatives blitzed the Internet with the suggestion that Obama might not be an American citizen. Doubt was cast on either of his parents being American citizens. The message went on to suggest that Obama refused to produce his birth certificate. All the while, Obama was traveling abroad on a US passport, a document that cannot be obtained without a US birth certificate.

Considering that the [2008] Republican [presidential] candidate, John McCain, was born in the Panama Canal Zone, only the GOP [Grand Old Party, or Republican Party] would be dumb enough to make an issue over whether the Democrats' candidate was born in one of the 50 states.

The innuendo and negativism with which the Republicans are conducting their presidential campaign are unprecedented. There is no sign of issues in McCain's Karl Rovian [referring to Republican political strategist and President Bush's top adviser Karl Rove] campaign. Issues have been superseded by hate, lies, and war.

Republicans stand for war without end, a police state to make us "safe," and "energy independence," which means drilling for oil in the Arctic National Wildlife Refuge and offshore of Florida's Gulf Coast beaches.

Translation of Terms

What Republicans really mean by "energy independence" is prevailing over environmentalists. Republicans lump environmentalists in the same category with abortionists, gays, feminists, food stamp recipients, trade unionists and terrorists. To a Republican, saving America means prevailing over these people.

The notion that Americans can achieve energy independence by drilling offshore wells and in the Arctic is absurd. A number of experts have pointed out that the best data do not support any such possibility.

For example, Robert Kaufman at Boston University, citing US government data, reports that the US might have 40 billion barrels of oil in undeveloped reserves which are not off-limits. Another 19 billion might be in off-limit offshore sites and in the Arctic National Wildlife Refuge.

All of this oil cannot be brought up at once, and apparently none before 2017. Bringing it all into production would, experts think, increase US oil production by 1–4 percent. In other words, nothing. Currently the US uses 21 million barrels a day, and the entire world uses 86 million barrels a day. At best, the Arctic National Wildlife Refuge could by 2017 produce 1 million barrels a day, about one-twentieth of current US use and one-eighty-sixth of current world use.

This is not energy independence, and it would have no material effect on price. Indeed, the offshoring by US corporations of US jobs has a much greater effect on the dollar price

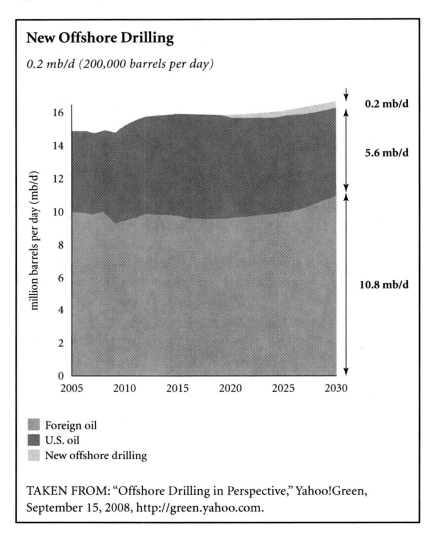

New Offshore Drilling

0.2 mb/d (200,000 barrels per day)

0.2 mb/d

5.6 mb/d

10.8 mb/d

Foreign oil
U.S. oil
New offshore drilling

TAKEN FROM: "Offshore Drilling in Perspective," Yahoo!Green, September 15, 2008, http://green.yahoo.com.

of oil by inflating the US trade deficit and driving down the exchange value of the US dollar. But, of course, here we are talking about facts, and facts are of no interest to Republicans.

Republicans are interested in prevailing over the "bad guys." The fact that the bad guys are [former president George W.] Bush, [former vice president Dick] Cheney, [former secretary of state Condoleezza] Rice, [former deputy secretary of defense Paul] Wolfowitz, [former chairman of the Defense

Policy Board Richard] Perle, [*Weekly Standard* editor] Billy Kristol, and other such is beyond the Republicans' imagination. Bad guys are "towel heads" with beards and robes and are "over there" where they must be killed before they come "over here." The extent of the Republican intellect boils down to "over here" vs. "over there."

> "A 21st-century energy policy must ra-
> tionally encourage innovation and con-
> servation, and pay attention to the en-
> vironmental impact of our choices as
> well. And if you want oil prices to de-
> cline, drill."

Offshore Drilling Will Lower Energy Prices

Kevin A. Hassett

Kevin A. Hassett is a senior fellow and the director of economic policy studies at the American Enterprise Institute for Public Policy Research (AEI). In the following viewpoint, he contends that by increasing offshore exploration and drilling, the United States would be encouraging oil-producing nations to put more oil on the market now, thereby lowering oil prices on the world- wide market. Hassett concludes that if you want oil prices to de- crease, offshore drilling is an important part of the equation.

As you read, consider the following questions:

1. According to the U.S. Department of the Interior, how many billions of barrels of recoverable oil are in the nation's Outer Continental Shelf?

Kevin A. Hassett, "Start Drilling Now to Lower Oil, Gasoline Prices," Bloomberg.com, July 28, 2008, p. Commentary. Copyright © 2008 Bloomberg L.P. All rights reserved. Used with permission.

2. How many billions of barrels of oil did the United States produce in 2007?

3. How many billions of barrels of oil did the United States consume in 2007?

High energy prices have everyone who doesn't own an oil well in the dumps. Consumer sentiment is the lowest it has been in almost 30 years, and a recent analysis of sentiment by Economy.com suggests that high gas prices are the main culprit.

Against this backdrop, it is hardly surprising that politicians are debating ways to reduce energy prices.

To Drill or Not to Drill?

The two sides are as far apart as can be. Republicans have argued that, in addition to aggressively seeking alternatives to oil, we should work to develop new reserves at home. Democrats, for the most part, have argued that oil discoveries can't affect the current high price, because any newly discovered reserves take so long to deliver.

Barack Obama, the presumptive Democratic presidential nominee, summarized this argument concisely recently, when he said: "Offshore drilling would not lower gas prices today, it would not lower gas prices next year and it would not lower gas prices five years from now."

Who is right? The economics of natural resources clearly favors the Republican view.

The economics of extracting resources is quite simple and intuitive. If you own property that has oil in the ground, then you have to decide how rapidly you wish to deplete your resource. If prices are low today, and you expect them to be much higher in the future, then you will hold off pumping a lot.

Open Spigot Now

If prices are high today and are expected to be much lower tomorrow, then you would rather open up the spigot now when profits will be higher.

If exploration can be expected to be successful and significantly increase oil production in the future, then it would cause producers to revise downward their estimates for future prices. This would increase the attractiveness of extracting more today. As producers respond with higher production, prices today would drop.

The argument that drilling wouldn't influence today's price rests on two possible assertions. The first is that exploration will fail. In that case, estimates of future prices would be unaffected by discoveries that won't happen. The second is that current producers wouldn't look ahead to lower future prices and increase supply today to maximize profits.

Both assertions are clearly false.

Low-Ball Estimate

According to the U.S. Department of the Interior, there are about 86 billion barrels of recoverable oil in the nation's Outer Continental Shelf. Since government agencies tend to be conservative on such matters, this estimate may well be low.

To put that cache of oil in perspective, in 2007, the United States produced about 3 billion barrels of oil and consumed more than 7-1/2 billion. The potential undiscovered haul is more than 10 times our annual consumption. It is inconceivable that extraction from such large reserves would have no effect on future prices.

What about prices today? A vast body of academic literature finds that future prices and spot prices are intricately linked in a manner that could only occur if producers are constantly updating their plans based on expected prices.

Offshore Drilling and Prices

If you don't believe American drilling can affect prices, consider what Chakib Khelil, the Algerian minister for Energy and Mines and president of OPEC [Organization of the Petroleum Exporting Countries], said today (July 1 [2008]) in Madrid at the World Petroleum Congress. Asked by an American reporter about what measures the United States could take to help lower oil prices, he suggested that the United States needs to stabilize the value of the dollar. And then he said, "Open up your exploration. In Algeria, we have a bidding round [for new oil exploration licenses] going on. We are open. The United States also needs to open—offshore Florida; offshore Alaska need to be opened to exploration."

Americans love to hate OPEC. But when the head of OPEC says the United States should drill more to help increase supplies, and therefore lower prices, perhaps American politicians—and that means the Democrats— should pay attention.

Robert Bryce,
"The Democrats and Off-Shore Drilling,"
CounterPunch, *July 2, 2008.*

A recent study by economists Param Silvapulle and Imad Moosa of Monash University in Australia found strong evidence of what is called bidirectional causality. Future prices and spot prices are inextricably linked.

Too Obvious

How strong is the case? My American Enterprise Institute [for Public Policy Research] colleague, former U.S. House Speaker Newt Gingrich, has been a tireless advocate of a more rational energy policy that allows for more drilling.

In a recent post at his influential blog, Gingrich noted that the top academic energy journal, aptly named the *Energy Journal*, recently rejected a study by economists Morris Coats and Gary Pecquet of Nicholls State University in Louisiana that found that higher production in the future would reduce prices today.

The study, Gingrich reported, wasn't rejected because it lacked academic merit. It was rejected because the finding was so well known. James Smith, the impeccably credentialed editor of the *Energy Journal* described it this way to the unfortunate authors:

> "Basically, your main result (the present impact of an anticipated future supply change) is already known to economists (although perhaps not to the Democratic Policy Committee [DPC]). It is our policy to publish only original research that adds significantly to the body of received knowledge regarding energy markets and policy."

A 21st-century energy policy must rationally encourage innovation and conservation, and pay attention to the environmental impact of our choices as well. And if you want oil prices to decline, drill.

> *"New drilling is contentious for a variety of reasons, but the most obvious argument against it is that neither the size nor anticipated rate of new domestic production will be sufficient to alter the price of oil on the global market by more than a few cents."*

Offshore Drilling Will Not Significantly Lower Energy Prices

Bryan K. Mignone

Bryan K. Mignone is the director of research on the Energy Security Initiative and a fellow at the Brookings Institution. In the following viewpoint, he points out that studies have shown that increasing offshore exploration and drilling will not significantly lower oil prices. Mignone argues that the only real way to lower oil prices is to develop alternative sources of fuel.

As you read, consider the following questions:

1. According to a recent study, how much domestic revenue would be generated by offshore drilling in restricted areas?

Bryan K. Mignone, "Drilling Our Way to the Future," *The Hill*, September 24, 2008. Copyright © 2008 Capitol Hill Publishing Corp. Reproduced by permission.

2. Why does the author believe that offshore drilling does not accomplish the aims of a comprehensive energy policy?

3. Why does the author state that the current debate over offshore drilling is merely a "distraction"?

With the fallout from Wall Street firmly positioned at the top of the congressional agenda this week [September 24, 2008], it may be convenient to forget that the fate of bipartisan energy legislation also hangs in the balance.

Last week, the House considered a measure to partially lift offshore drilling bans in exchange for increases in the financial incentives for renewable energy. The final vote in favor—by a margin of 236–189—effectively handed the legislative baton over to the Senate.

Even if the House-passed bill ultimately fails to garner a vote in the other chamber as this final, tightly constrained session draws to a close, the Senate may still be forced to confront this complex set of issues in another form. Senate leaders will almost certainly face strong pressure to let drilling bans expire in the so-called continuing resolution—the critical piece of budget legislation that maintains federal spending beyond the end of the fiscal year. They have also been considering financial incentives separately as part of a larger tax package.

The Energy Debate

This odd state of affairs begs an obvious question: Is drilling worth yet another fight and yet more gridlock around energy?

New drilling is contentious for a variety of reasons, but the most obvious argument against it is that neither the size nor anticipated rate of new domestic production will be sufficient to alter the price of oil on the global market by more than a few cents.

For all of the negatives, however, drilling does come with one obvious benefit: It shifts a greater share of oil revenue from international to domestic suppliers, meaning that a greater fraction of oil expenditures would accrue to U.S. firms rather than to regimes with interests openly hostile to ours.

In fact, in one recent study, Robert W. Hahn of the American Enterprise Institute [for Public Policy Research] and Peter Passell of the Milken Institute project that even the relatively small contribution from currently restricted areas could add up to more than $1.85 trillion in new domestic revenue, whereas the environmental costs would amount to perhaps $400 million. The seemingly simple conclusion is that new drilling makes economic sense, even if the net benefits go undetected by most.

Drilling Does Not Equal Comprehensive Energy Policy

The problem with stopping there, of course, is that drilling, on its own, achieves none of the real objectives of a comprehensive energy policy. Most notably, it fails to address the problem that motivates such policies in the first place—high energy costs—because, for reasons already mentioned, the impact of our supply contribution is simply too small to significantly change the global price of oil.

A drilling-only policy falls short on several other grounds as well: It would not insulate consumers from price shocks, since the share of oil used in our economy would not decrease; it would not significantly lessen the global transfer of wealth to exporting nations, since our decreased contribution to this transfer would be relatively small on a global scale; and it would not mitigate the threat of global climate change, because carbon dioxide emissions would not decrease.

Encourage Alternate Fuels

Despite the obvious barriers, the only plausible solution to this larger and more difficult set of issues is to gradually displace the oil used in transportation, and the only way to do this is to make investments in technology alternatives more

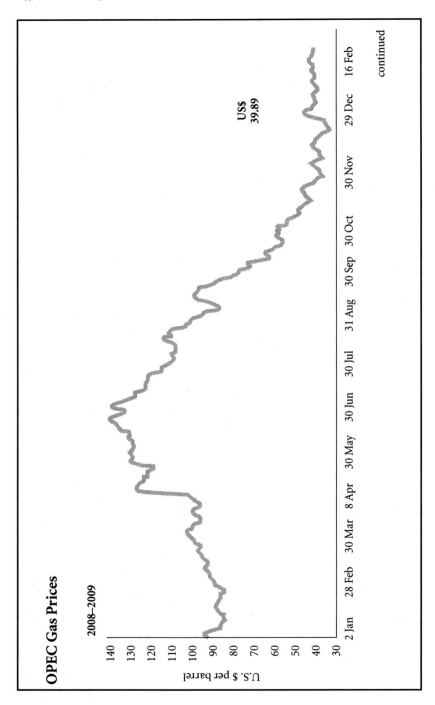

OPEC Gas Prices

2008–2009

US$ 39.89

U.S. $ per barrel

140 130 120 110 100 90 80 70 60 50 40 30

2 Jan 28 Feb 30 Mar 8 Apr 30 May 30 Jun 30 Jul 31 Aug 30 Sep 30 Oct 30 Nov 29 Dec 16 Feb

continued

OPEC Gas Prices [CONTINUED]

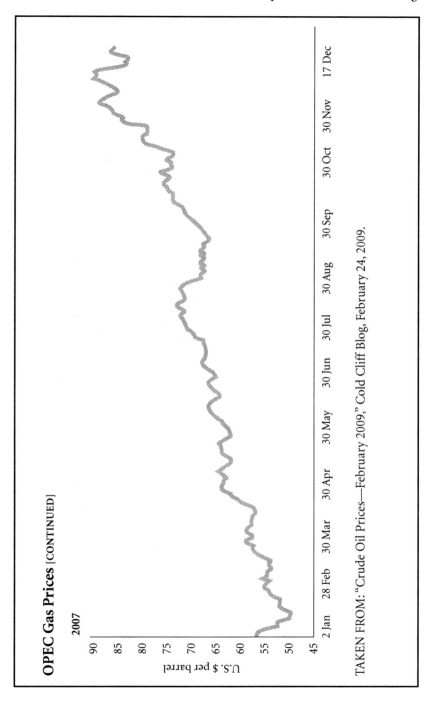

TAKEN FROM: "Crude Oil Prices—February 2009," Cold Cliff Blog, February 24, 2009.

attractive. Given the diverse set of policies needed to bring about such transformation—from providing incentives for plug-in hybrids to reforming the grid in ways that would accommodate the push toward electrification—the disproportionate emphasis on a drilling policy whose impacts would scarcely be noticeable at all is merely a distraction.

But, for better or worse, the resolution to the House debate suggests that the now-fashionable do-it-all approach may be the political compromise through which some of these more important objectives can ultimately be achieved, at least in the waning hours of this Congress. That's not really such a bad deal, if one believes that exchanging something that doesn't matter for something that does is a decant bargain.

So, as strange as it sounds, perhaps it is possible to start drilling our way to a clean energy future.

> *"If Congress adopted a comprehensive plan to open up domestic oil production in the U.S., everyone would know that in the long run the price of oil would be heading down."*

An Offshore Drilling Moratorium Is an Assault on the Living Standard of the Middle Class

Peter Ferrara

Peter Ferrara is director of entitlement and budget policy at the Institute for Policy Innovation and general counsel of the American Civil Rights Union. In the following viewpoint, Ferrara asserts that liberals have shut down new offshore oil exploration and drilling by using environmental regulations and filing lawsuits. Ferrara also points out that the Barack Obama administration "thinks truth and justice requires a reduction in our opulent middle-class living standards."

As you read, consider the following questions:

1. How long was Seabrook Station held up by regulatory delays, according to the author?

Peter Ferrara, "Shut Up and Produce Some Oil," *The American Spectator*, July 23, 2008. Copyright © The American Spectator 2008. Reproduced by permission.

2. When does the author say the last oil and gas refinery was built in the United States?

3. According to the author, when could oil wells off the Pacific Coast be producing if the United States put them back online?

Liberals are flailing about looking for some political cover on energy and gas prices. For decades now, they have supported the policies of extremists who have systematically sought to shut down every major energy source for our economy. We can't drill for oil offshore, we can't drill in the frozen tundra of north Alaska, we can't even develop oil shale on the mainland. Liberals are even opposing the development of new oil discoveries in the Plains states. Meanwhile, China is now producing oil from wells in Cuban waters off the coast of Florida, selling and reaping enormous profits from oil that America should be producing.

No New Nuclear Power

Nuclear power? Can't have that. Jane Fonda showed us in a movie in the 1970s how dangerous that is. France and Japan have produced most of their electricity for decades through the nuclear power technology that America developed, and they are now competing to sell nuclear plant development to China and India.

One of the last U.S. nuclear projects was the Shoreham plant begun by Long Island Lighting Company in 1973. After years of ridiculous regulatory delays, the plant was shut down in 1989 by protests by liberal flower children, before producing any electricity. Long Island Lighting went bankrupt as a result. New Hampshire's Seabrook Station was held up for 14 years by similar regulatory delays, before finally opening in 1990 (and operating without harm ever since).

This is why there has been no new nuclear plant construction in the U.S. since then. Those regulatory delays are due to laws and policies adopted by liberals, who are willing to let extremists use them to shut down any such construction.

Liberals Oppose Coal-Fired Electric Plants

Liberals are now even opposing the development and even the maintenance of coal-fired electric plants. The energy policy statement on [presidential candidate] Barack Obama's Web site says, "Obama believes that the imperative to confront climate change requires that we prevent a new wave of traditional coal facilities in the U.S." In Georgia, a state judge denied a permit for a new coal electricity plant on the grounds of global warming (which is a figment of the liberal imagination to justify a big government power grab). Meanwhile, China opens a new coal plant every week on its way to eventually pass the U.S. as the number one economy in the world.

The last new oil and gas refinery was built in the U.S. in 1976. A good example of the reason why is going on right now in Indiana. BP is constructing a $3.8 billion expansion of its already existing Whiting Refinery in that state. But the Natural Resources Defense Council (NRDC) has now brought suit against BP seeking an injunction against the expansion, and fines of $32,500 for each day construction has been under way. The NRDC is urging the court to adopt a new interpretation of state law that would require BP to get a new state permit first because with the expansion, the refinery would supposedly discharge more "pollution" than the current state permit allows. If the NRDC has found a liberal enough judge, it may get its way, to the great detriment of the rest of us.

Some liberals are even now calling for the elimination of already built and operating hydroelectric power plants, on the grounds that the dams in such projects distort the environment too much. This would require dams to be destroyed and occupied valleys to be flooded.

Demand for Energy Is Growing

The problem for liberals is that we are now running into the iron logic of the law of supply and demand, which, unfortunately for them, most voters can understand. Shut down the supply of oil and you get gas prices starting to run towards $5 a gallon. This winter [2008–09] the price of home heating oil will brutalize the budgets of many families. We are getting to the point where an effective bumper sticker will be "Keep the Lights on, Vote Republican."

That is why the bold Republican initiative to expand oil production and other energy supplies, originally developed by Newt Gingrich, is so effective, and so threatening, to liberals. Polls show increasingly overwhelming public support.

As a result, liberals are flailing about offering increasingly absurd distractions. One argument is that even if we started drilling for oil now, we wouldn't get any increased supply, and any reduction in gas prices, for 10 years or more. One popinjay from the misnamed Center for American Progress was recently spouting on TV that there would be no effect until 2030.

Prices Speak for Themselves

Well, let's see. On Friday, July 14 [2008], the price of a barrel of oil hit $147. On Monday, July 17, President [George W.] Bush withdrew the executive order banning offshore drilling. That doesn't even start any new drilling because there is still a congressional ban in place. Nevertheless, by Friday, July 21, after 4 straight days of decline, the price of oil had plummeted to $128, a decline of 13% on a symbolic action alone. The Center for American "Progress" was only off by 21 years, 51 weeks.

There are oil wells off the Pacific Coast that were capped years ago when the offshore drilling ban was first adopted. They could be brought back into production in less than a year. Expert oil engineers recently interviewed have said other sites could be producing in 18 months. The standard estimate for production from new drilling in Alaska is 10 years. But if the government gets the lawsuits and regulatory delays out of the way, here's betting the new wells would be producing in less than 5 years.

More importantly, if Congress adopted a comprehensive plan to open up domestic oil production in the U.S., everyone would know that in the long run the price of oil would be heading down. That would break the back of the oil panic today that has driven the price up to ridiculous levels. If the Fed [Federal Reserve] reversed its weak dollar policy at the same time, within a year the price of oil would drop by 50% or more, dropping the price of gas down close to $2 a gallon, which is where it should be. In a competitive market, price is supposed to equal the marginal cost of production. For a barrel of oil, that would be $25 to $40 at most, which is where the long-term price of oil would be if the U.S. removed production restrictions.

World Supply of Oil Is Central Factor

Another distraction is the argument that even if new oil production is allowed, there is no guarantee the oil companies won't sell the oil to Japan or China rather than to American consumers. This argument is 100% bad economics. The truth is, *it doesn't matter where the oil is sold.* All the new production would increase the world supply of oil regardless of where it is sold. With world supply up, the world price would decline. If new production from Alaska is sold to Japan, the oil that would have otherwise been sold to Japan could then be sold to the U.S.

In fact, if you look at a globe, you would see that Alaska is close to Japan. It would be most efficient, meaning reduced costs and prices, for the production there to be sold to Japan, and for production from South America that would otherwise go to Japan to go to the U.S. instead. That would be the natu-

"We'll be there soon, dear. Your dad will only be pushing us until gas prices go down." Cartoon by Jerry King. www.CartoonStock.com.

ral result of an efficient market. But to counter the distracting nonsense of desperate liberals grasping for power at all costs, the new production can always be required to be sold in the U.S.

Still another distracting argument is that the oil companies already have millions of acres in oil leases, so why don't they just produce more oil from those areas? The oil companies pay for those leases for exploration. There is no guarantee that any leased areas will actually hold producible oil. Given that the oil companies must pay rent for the term of those leases regardless of whether any oil is produced, and that the price of oil is at record, unprecedented, historic levels, any oil company that was not producing all it could from any of its leases would be subject to shareholder lawsuits for waste of corporate assets. It is just like liberals to demand that oil companies produce more from areas that do not hold any more oil while denying access to areas with massive proven reserves.

More Distractions from the Real Issue

Liberals argue that if we would just sell a small portion of the oil from the Strategic Petroleum Reserve that the U.S. government holds in case of emergency, oil and gas prices would fall. So now all of a sudden liberals recognize that increased supply on the market would reduce prices. But any such sales would be a drop in the bucket, and only temporary, likely, indeed, to be reversed later to restore the reserve. So this would have no significant, lasting effect.

Yet another distraction is that we should just increase the required miles per gallon under the CAFE [Corporate Average Fuel Economy] standards for the production of new vehicles. This is no answer to the oil and gas price problem because it involves only restricting consumer freedom of choice, and ultimately reducing the American standard of living. It means that consumers should be prohibited from buying the vehicles they want, and instead should be allowed to buy only the vehicles the government wants them to have. The SUV [sport-utility vehicle] explosion was all about the American consumer wanting bigger, more powerful vehicles rather than vehicles with better fuel economy. There have long been low-cost vehicles available for sale in the United States operating with close to 50 miles per gallon in fuel efficiency. But consumers have failed to choose those cars, while close to half of sales of new vehicles have been SUVs with low fuel efficiency exempt from the CAFE standards.

If now with higher gas prices American consumers want to abandon SUVs and buy more fuel-efficient cars, that should be their choice. But the government should not be imposing that choice on them. Yet Barack Obama says on his Web site that he wants "to double fuel economy standards within 18 years." That involves an assault on the standard of living of the middle class, which would be forced to give up the big, powerful vehicles they now enjoy for the tiny, little sardine cans that most Europeans drive. In fact, there has been talk precisely of allowing car manufacturers to import into the United States the little fuel-efficient vehicles that they now make for Europe.

Marie Antoinette School

Assaulting the standard of living of the middle class is what Barack Obama is all about. For you can search through all of his position papers, speeches and talking points and not find a word about reducing the price of gas or oil. He clearly has no intention of trying to reduce the price of gas at all. He has said, in fact, that the high price of gas and oil is good for the environment, and the only problem is that the prices increased too suddenly. This is the Marie Antoinette [queen of France known for her extravagant lifestyle while the people suffered] school of energy policy.

Remember Obama's famous quote:

"We can't just keep driving our SUVs, eating whatever we want, keeping our homes at 72 degrees at all times regardless of whether we live in the tundra or the desert, and keep consuming 25 percent of the world's resources with just 4 percent of the world's population, and expect the rest of the world to say you just go ahead. We'll be fine. That's not leadership. That's not going to happen."

What he means by this is that the current standard of living of the American people is unfair. It represents massive inequality in comparison to the rest of the world. So here we have a leading presidential candidate who thinks truth and justice requires a reduction in our opulent middle-class living standards. Good luck, and good night.

> "It is irresponsible to allow companies that escaped the payment of potentially more than $60 billion in royalties because of a loophole to get access to more leases."

Offshore Drilling Will Enrich Big Oil Companies and Hurt the Middle Class

Tyson Slocum

Tyson Slocum is the director of Public Citizen's Energy Program. In the following viewpoint, he reports that a number of oil companies have been allowed to escape paying royalties on oil and natural gas extracted from U.S. territory in the Gulf of Mexico. Slocum argues that if these freeloading companies are allowed to bid on new leases, the oil companies will get richer and leave the American people holding the bag.

As you read, consider the following questions:

1. How much money does the author assert oil companies have gotten out of paying the U.S. government?

2. How many oil companies have avoided paying these royalties?

Tyson Slocum, "Oil Companies Escape Billions in Royalty Payments to Americans," Public Citizen, July 30, 2008. Reproduced by permission.

3. Which four companies does the author cite as having signed a voluntary agreement to repay these royalties?

A bureaucratic oversight has allowed 24 oil companies to avoid more than $1.3 billion in royalties for the privilege of extracting oil and natural gas from U.S. territory in the Gulf of Mexico—with foreign companies responsible for 55 percent of that total. But this $1.3 billion in forgone royalties pales in comparison to the $60 billion that Americans stand to lose in royalty revenue over the life of these leases. And if Congress repeals the moratorium on Outer Continental Shelf (OCS) drilling that has existed since 1982, these freeloading oil companies will be eligible to bid on new leases, providing them with more record profits while American families are left holding the bag. These 24 companies have posted a combined $365 billion in profits since 2006.

The list of the specific companies comes from a February 2008 U.S. Department of the Interior memo recently obtained by Public Citizen. Four of the 24 companies (BP, Marathon, Shell and Walter Oil & Gas) signed voluntary agreements to pay royalties going forward, but they will not be required to pay the more than $200 million taxpayers have been denied on production that already has occurred.

The U.S. Senate is currently considering amendments to the Stop Excessive Energy Speculation Act of 2008 (S. 3268) that would repeal the congressional ban on offshore drilling. The U.S. House of Representatives is also considering measures in the Deep Ocean Energy Resources Act of 2008 (H.R. 6108) that would open up the OCS to new drilling. However, allowing new drilling in these areas will not significantly lower gasoline prices. According to a U.S. Department of Energy report, opening all areas off the coast of the Atlantic, Pacific and the Gulf of Mexico to new drilling "would not have a significant impact on domestic crude oil and natural gas production or prices before 2030." And new areas were opened for drilling in December 2006, when Congress passed the Gulf of Mexico

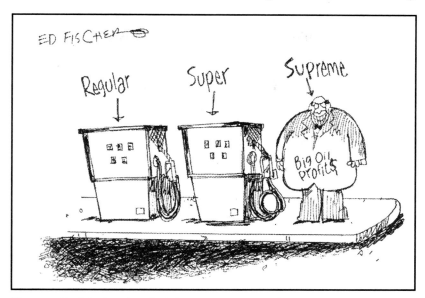

"Supreme Gas." Cartoon by Ed Fischer. www.CartoonStock.com.

Energy Security Act (Public Law 109-432), which authorized leasing 8.3 million acres in the Gulf of Mexico, 70 percent of which had been previously protected under congressional moratoria.

Time for Oil Companies to Act Responsibly

It is irresponsible to allow companies that escaped the payment of potentially more than $60 billion in royalties because of a loophole to get a access to more leases. There is legislative precedent to force companies to pay their fair share. The House passed a measure in January 2007 that would forbid oil companies from being awarded any new leases unless they renegotiate non-royalty leases from 1998 and 1999. President [George W.] Bush opposed this part of the legislation, and the Senate has yet to adopt it. The United States is the third-largest producer of oil in the world, and 31 percent of that production comes from land owned by the federal government.

It should not come as a surprise that much of the impetus for opening the OCS comes from an expensive advertising campaign financed by former House Speaker Newt Gingrich's American Solutions for Winning the Future. When Gingrich was Speaker, Congress passed the Deep Water Royalty Relief Act of 1995. It turned out to be an even bigger favor than Congress had intended.

Companies Ripping off American Citizens

Because of a bureaucratic oversight by the Department of the Interior during the implementation of the act, oil companies that secured leases in 1998 and 1999 were exempted from royalties, regardless of the prevailing market price of oil. This stands in stark contrast to other, similar leases, which require the payment of royalties if the price of oil exceeds a certain threshold. The day the bill was signed in November 1995, West Texas Intermediate oil was trading at $18.28/barrel. With oil now trading nearly 600 percent higher at more than $120/barrel, these companies have been and will be extracting very valuable energy from public land without paying any royalties to American taxpayers.

In addition, there is widespread mismanagement of the royalty program that allows oil companies to underpay royalties, resulting in Americans being cheated out of hundreds of millions of dollars. Unless that is fixed, expansion of OCS development will also unfairly enrich oil companies, most of which are foreign. A former top auditor at the Department of the Interior testified under oath in March 2007 that his superiors limited his ability to collect royalties from oil companies that were owed to the American people. In 2007, a jury in a case filed under the False Claims Act found that Kerr-McGee (now Anadarko), one of the holders of the no-royalty leases from 1998 and 1999, deliberately underpaid more than $7.5 million in royalties.

> *"For those who accept that burning fossil fuels is contributing to climate change and that there are finite limits to the amount of* inexpensive *oil that can be pumped out of the earth, a new offshore oil rush is a psychological and practical disaster."*

Offshore Drilling Will Accelerate Global Warming

Andrew Leonard

Andrew Leonard is a staff writer at Salon.com, focusing on science and technology issues. In the following viewpoint, Leonard maintains that increasing the practice of offshore oil drilling will ensure the continued burning of fossil fuels, which will accelerate global warming. It is far more preferable, he argues, to limit offshore oil and keep the price of gas high, thereby forcing Americans to innovate and transition to alternative sources of fuel.

As you read, consider the following questions:

1. According to a 2007 report by the U.S. Minerals Management Service, how many oil spills were caused by hurricanes Rita and Katrina?

Andrew Leonard, "Slick John McCain and the Offshore Oil Ruse," Salon.com, June 25, 2008. This article first appeared in Salon.com, at http://www.salon.com. An online version remains in the Salon archives. Reprinted with permission.

2. How many gallons of oil were spilled because of hurricanes Rita and Katrina?

3. How many gallons of oil were spilled in the Santa Barbara disaster of 1969?

An example of leadership or reckless chutzpah? On Monday [June 23, 2008], [Republican presidential candidate] John McCain visited Santa Barbara [California], the scene of one of the great environmental disasters in American history, and proceeded to downplay the potential consequences of lifting the federal moratorium on new offshore drilling. Modern drilling technology is environmentally safe, he told the audience. According to the Associated Press, McCain "cited the examples of Louisiana and Texas, noting they have allowed drilling and weathered two devastating hurricanes with minimal or no oil spills."

McCain exaggerated. A 2007 report by the U.S. Minerals Management Service unearthed by *Outside the Beltway* documented the damage caused in the Gulf of Mexico by hurricanes Katrina and Rita: "124 spills were reported with a total volume of roughly 17,700 barrels of total petroleum products."

Now, 17,700 barrels of oil equals 743,400 gallons. Whether you consider that a lot or a little depends on your perspective. Compared with the 1.5 million barrels pumped out of the Gulf *every day*, it is a trivial amount. But it's also within shouting distance of the 3 million gallons of oil spilled in the Santa Barbara offshore oil disaster of 1969.

That spill is considered the "environmental shot heard 'round the world." The catastrophe crystallized the environmental movement into a potent political force, resulting in the quick passage of the National Environmental Protection Act later that year, the creation of the EPA [Environmental Protection Agency] in 1970 and, ultimately, the ban on new offshore drilling.

The Real Issue

But the safety of offshore drilling is a distraction from what's really at issue in the current tussle over energy policy. An oil spill here or there is irrelevant to the much larger challenges that humanity faces: climate change and peak oil.

The truth is, we can probably make offshore drilling as safe as we reasonably want it to be. Norway, with its environmentally aware citizenry and tight coordination between a watchful government and a state-owned oil company, has been drilling for decades in the North Sea with reasonably good environmental results (notwithstanding the spillage of 24,000 barrels of oil just last December [2007]). Then again, for an example of how it can all go terribly wrong, visit Nigeria, where lax environmental controls have resulted in a huge mess in the Niger Delta, and where rebel forces attacked an offshore oil platform just this week.

But drilling practices and technology have improved. With the appropriate government oversight and regulation, it may be possible to drill off the coasts of Florida and California without covering the beaches with sludge and killing thousands of seabirds. Provided we acknowledge, of course, that a few nasty hurricanes in Florida will make at least a little bit of mess, and an earthquake in the wrong spot in California could be a slight problem. And provided we are capable of following the example of Norway, where the government and the people tell the oil company what to do, rather than the example set by the current [George W.] Bush administration, where the energy industry is in charge of policy making.

But drilling for more oil in the United States will not lower the price of gas in the short term—even McCain admitted as much when he said on Monday, "I don't see an immediate relief, [but] the fact that we are exploiting those reserves would have [a] psychological impact that I think is beneficial." Bush's own Department of Energy concluded in 2004 that the long-term impact of lifting the moratorium on offshore drilling on oil prices would be "insignificant." The only way that expanded drilling, offshore and in ANWR [Arctic National Wildlife Refuge], could make a difference at the pump is if global production of oil started significantly outpacing the growth of global demand. Which would probably require that Saudi Arabia crank open the spigot and China, India, and the rest of the world's rapidly emerging economies start to lose their enormous thirst.

In other words, not only is it unlikely, it is completely out of our hands.

New Offshore Drilling Will Accelerate Climate Change

For those who accept that burning fossil fuels is contributing to climate change and that there are finite limits to the amount of *inexpensive* oil that can be pumped out of the earth, a new offshore oil rush is a psychological and practical disaster. It would accelerate climate change and, in the unlikely scenario that new drilling even momentarily slowed down global oil price appreciation, would still postpone that inevitable day of reckoning with the even higher fossil fuel energy prices sure to arrive.

The longer we wait to deal with either problem, the more painful and expensive our options for coping with these challenges will become and the more constrained our maneuvering room will be. The sorry truth is that from the perspective of grappling with climate change, and encouraging investment into alternative energy technologies, expensive gas now is far preferable to even more expensive gas later.

Deniers Blame Environmentalists

Of course, there are plenty of people, mostly on the right wing of the political spectrum in the United States, who do not accept that climate change is real or caused by human in-

"Ocean sounds will not be heard. Instead, here's an ad for investment opportunities in offshore drilling." Cartoon by Harley Schwadron. www.CartoonStock.com.

dustrial activity, and who believe there are no real constraints to the global oil supply. They'd prefer to blame environmental activists, present-day descendants of the rabid left-wing Commies who exploited the Santa Barbara spill to pursue their antibusiness agenda, for today's "high" gas prices.

Such accusations are the stuff of daily grandstanding rhetoric from congressional Republicans and constitute a major, long-standing front in the culture wars.

There's a large contingent of Americans who do acknowledge that global warming is real and that it would be smart to consume less oil. But the prospect of $5 gasoline tends to reduce their focus from the long term to the here-and-now. The oceans haven't flooded their homes just yet, but their pocketbooks are hurting today.

And there's an election campaign going on.

Issue of Offshore Drilling and the Election

In Las Vegas on Tuesday [June 24, 2008], [Democratic presidential candidate] Barack Obama delivered a significant speech on energy issues. He criticized McCain's proposal for new offshore drilling and commented that McCain's reference to "psychological impact" is "Washington-speak for 'it polls well.'" No joke.

In Santa Barbara, McCain attempted to assuage Californian sensitivities by saying that his real position on the moratorium on offshore drilling is that it should fall under the rubric of "state's rights"—meaning that if Californians want to keep their coastline pristine, they will have the power to do so under a McCain administration. But McCain knows he's not going to win California, so it doesn't matter what he says in Santa Barbara. The offshore oil ploy is a calculated gambit aimed at cashing in on the pain that economically stressed voters in swing states far from the coast (as well as Florida, where environmental sensitivities seem to be on less solid ground than in California) are feeling. In Ohio and Michigan, the ugliness of oil derricks blotting out the sunset isn't a number one problem on anyone's priority list.

McCain's goal is to marry the antienvironmentalist Republican base with the I-like-the-environment-but-am-economically-hurting moderates. Call it the coalition of the unwilling to pay high gas prices.

In his speech, Obama set forth a pretty straightforward platform of vastly increased investment in renewable energy, conservation and efficiency, and proposed to ease the pain of working class Americans with an economic stimulus plan. One can question how he would end up paying for his proposals or whether he will succeed in steering them through Congress, but one thing that must be conceded is that his approach represents a clear difference from McCain.

McCain's Energy Policies

Suppose that McCain's strategy works. Suppose voters in enough swing states decide that the pain of high gas prices is so great that they will go with the candidate who is promising them the easy way out—the gas tax holiday and offshore drilling and a nuclear power plant in every pot. What will that tell us about the American ability to suck it up and face down the challenges of the future?

Easy. It will tell us that we've lost the battle before we've hardly begun to fight. It will tell us that the environment is toast. We will have established that we, the citizens of the richest and most powerful country on the earth, are unwilling to pay the price necessary for embarking on a long-term ecologically sustainable path for existence on the planet. If $4 gasoline is enough incentive to lift the moratorium on offshore drilling, then $10-a-gallon gasoline will inspire even more drastic consequences. We will drill for every drop of oil, we will dig up every ounce of coal, we will sacrifice every environmental regulation, because we just can't take the heat. And then we'll fry.

It will also tell us that the environmental movement that took so much power from the Santa Barbara oil spill of 1969 has failed. That sustainability and conservation were luxuries we decided we could not afford.

"If you wanted to bring the United States to ruin, you could not have designed and implemented a more perfect scheme."

Offshore Drilling Will Not Accelerate Global Warming

Alan Caruba

Alan Caruba is a conservative commentator and an author. In the following viewpoint, he disputes the theory of global warming, arguing that evidence exists to disprove it. Caruba asserts that the rights of Americans to have access to cheap oil are more important than environmental considerations, which are often too limiting and politically motivated.

As you read, consider the following questions:

1. How many barrels of oil does the author estimate are in offshore areas?

2. How many barrels of oil does the author estimate are under government-owned land?

3. How many barrels of oil does the author estimate are under privately held land?

Alan Caruba, "Afloat on an Ocean of Oil," Intellectual Conservative, June 16, 2008. Copyright © 2008 Alan Caruba. Reproduced by permission of the author.

Considering how much untapped oil is known to exist, not just in the United States, but worldwide, one would think that its current price [in June 2008] was some kind of anomaly—and it is. It is more the result of speculation than anything else.

The most basic fact about oil worldwide is that there is lots of it. Though frequently overlooked, the ability to refine crude oil plays an essential role in the supply and demand equation. More refining capacity is needed worldwide. Finally, there's the fact that, in general, oil is very expensive to get at and [is] often found in the most inhospitable places on earth.

Untapped Supply of Oil

For sheer insanity, however, consider a nation that has an estimated 31 billion barrels of oil offshore of its coasts and 117 billion barrels of oil under land owned or managed by the government, plus 139 billion barrels beneath privately held land.

In just one area, a desolate place designated a wildlife refuge, there's an estimated 7.7 billion barrels untapped. The nation with this abundance of oil is, of course, the United States of America. Most of the areas where oil is known to exist have been ruled off-limits to any exploration or extraction by the government.

In the areas where it is accessible, drilling for it is hugely encumbered and often denied by the National Environmental Policy Act [NEPA], the Clean Water Act [CWA], the Endangered Species Act [ESA], and the National Historic Preservation Act.

Environmental Regulations Killing
U.S. Energy Policy

If, however, you connect the dots, you will have noticed by now that America's energy problems, namely the price of a gallon of gasoline or heating oil, are making everyone miserable thanks in great part to environmental legislation designed to make it impossible to access oil on both public and privately held lands. Then, just to make matters worse, the government requires that every gallon of gasoline include the additive ethanol, which reduces mileage and increases its cost.

Further, we're told that [Democratic presidential candidate] senator Barack Obama, if elected, intends to seize "windfall profits." This is sufficient reason for American oil companies to decide to drill anywhere else. The last time a windfall profits tax was implemented was at the end of President [Jimmy] Carter's term. It had such a negative impact on U.S. oil companies that drilling for oil domestically dropped dramatically. It has stayed that way since the 1980s. Their actual profits are now less than pharmaceutical, high tech, and other elements of the economy. Imagine how thrilled they were to hear Rep. Maxine Waters's threat to nationalize them.

No profits. No exploration. No drilling. And no domestic oil with which to correct our dependence on foreign oil and thus provide a measure of security to a nation that runs on oil.

If you wanted to bring the United States to ruin, you could not have designed and implemented a more perfect scheme. Along with too many members of Congress, environmentalists are America's fifth column.

As my friend, Seldon B. Graham Jr., a veteran petroleum engineer and oil industry attorney and a graduate of West Point says of oil, "If it is worth dying for in the Near East, it is worth drilling for in the United States."

Myth of Dwindling Oil Supplies

As to the claim that the earth is running out of oil, that can be easily dismissed simply by reading information available in respected publications such as *BusinessWeek* that "the Saudis have embarked on an ambitious expansion program that

Myth of Global Warming

The recent record shows that the alleged global warming stopped in 1998 and it has been getting colder since, even if the warmist fanatics, in the face of the evidence, insist otherwise.

Button up your overcoat, Mr. [Al] Gore [environmental activist and former vice president]. It's going to get colder out there if Mother Nature has her way—and she always does.

Phil Brennan,
"Record Lows Dispel Global Warming Myths," NewsMax.com,
August 4, 2009. www.newsmax.com.

should see more than 2 million barrels of new production capacity come onstream by the middle of next year [2009]."

Those of us who follow energy trends read the *Energy Tribune* because it has some of the best information available on what is really occurring. In its May [2008] edition, Matt Pickard wrote about the expansion worldwide of offshore drilling, noting that today's prices are being driven by increased demand from rapidly developing nations such as China and India. This demand is going to increase over the next two or three decades.

Unless the United States begins to free up its own oil and natural gas reserves, Americans are going to be paying more at the pump and in their homes for a very long time to come.

Offshore Oil Is the Answer

The good news is that the offshore oil and gas industry, despite the huge risks and costs involved and despite an aging, understaffed workforce, is making strides to meet demand. Whether it's in the Gulf of Mexico or the North Sea, the icy waters of the Barents Sea or offshore of Brazil and Africa, massive new reserves of oil are being found.

"Large discoveries offshore Brazil, the continued progress in every region's major projects, and the ongoing push for Arctic exploration and production point to the industry's potential for growth over the next 20 to 30 years," wrote Pickard. Brazil is poised to become a major producer. In its Tupi [oil] field, "Petrobras announced an aggressive development plan, with an early production system possible within two or three years," reports Pickard. The nearby Jupiter field has gas reserves to rival Tupi.

None of this is a secret! Both privately owned U.S. and foreign national oil companies are going to find more oil and gas.

Alternative Energy Is Not the Answer

Neither candidate for president is telling the truth these days because both believe global warming is real and both keep blathering on about "alternative" energy. The big problem for the rest of us is that you can't pour wind or solar energy into a gas tank.

The U.S. mandate for ethanol as a gasoline additive has already significantly put the world's food supply in jeopardy, but most Americans are blissfully unaware that it requires 1.5 gallons of ethanol to produce the same energy as a gallon of gasoline. It actually emits more carbon dioxide than gasoline. It is an environmental hoax.

The world is afloat on an ocean of oil. Meanwhile, the United States continues to rule 85% of its offshore oil off-limits to exploration and extraction. This is occurring while the Chinese prepare to pump oil just offshore of Cuba, a mere 90 miles from Florida. It is occurring while the Russians are looking to plant their flag on potential reserves of subterranean oil in the Arctic.

Becoming Energy Independent

The next time you hear a politician say we need to be "energy independent," ask him or her why Americans cannot have access to the oil reserves known to exist in California, in Alaska, and in many of our other states or off the coastlines of Florida and elsewhere.

Ask them why the fate of the condors and little-known species is more important than the family budget of Americans forced to make choices between more food and more gasoline.

Ask them why they continue to claim that global warming is a threat when the entire Earth is now in a decade-old cooling cycle.

Ask them why they insist on blaming investor-owned oil companies whose own reserves are barely four percent of the world's known oil reserves? Ask them how they expect these oil companies to compete in the global marketplace when they threaten to seize their profits.

Energy is the master resource. It determines which nations thrive and which lag behind. For now, America is being ill-served by a Congress that refuses to permit access to our own energy resources.

Ask yourself how we have arrived at a point in time when both candidates for president believe in a nonexistent global warming and whose proposals offer no practical solution to our current and future energy needs.

Periodical Bibliography

The following articles have been selected to supplement the diverse views presented in this chapter.

James Abourezk	"Lies the Oil Companies Peddle," *Counter-Punch*, August 2, 2008.
Andrew Cline	"Big Oil Democrats," *American Spectator*, August 15, 2008.
Joe Conason	"On Energy, McCain Sounds a Lot Like Cheney," Salon.com, June 27, 2008. www.salon.com.
Peter Ferrara	"Shut Up and Produce Some Oil," *American Spectator*, July 23, 2008.
Karl Grossman	"Break Up Big Oil," *CounterPunch*, November 12, 2008.
Mark Hemingway	"Drilling in the Offshore," *National Review Online*, July 17, 2008. www.nationalreview.com.
Jacob Leibenluft	"What's the Deal with Offshore Drilling?" *Slate*, August 12, 2008.
Andrew Leonard	"Why Exxon Desperately Wants More Offshore Drilling," Salon.com, July 31, 2008. www.salon.com.
Jamie Reno	"The Lure of Black Gold," *Newsweek*, August 1, 2008. www.newsweek.com.
Bryan Walsh	"Will More Drilling Mean Cheaper Gas?" *TIME*, June 18, 2008.
David Weigel	"Shill Here, Shill Now," *Reason*, August 15, 2008.

OPPOSING
VIEWPOINTS®
SERIES

CHAPTER 3

What Offshore Drilling Policies Should the U.S. Government Consider?

Chapter Preface

With the Arctic Ocean to the north, the Pacific Ocean to the south, and the Bering Sea, Bering Strait, and Chukchi Sea to the west, Alaska is recognized as not only the largest U.S. state, but also the one with the longest coastline—in fact, it has more coastline than all of the other U.S. states combined. With that in mind, it is no surprise that Alaska has robust and lucrative fishing and tourist industries.

Alaska is also known for its oil and natural gas industry: It ranks second in the country for crude oil production. Oil accounts for most of the state's income, with most of the oil pumped from Alaska's North Slope oil fields and through the Trans-Alaska Pipeline. The most productive oil well in the North Slope is the Prudhoe Bay, covering approximately 214 acres and containing approximately 25 billion barrels of oil, making it the largest and most productive well in the United States.

Once heralded as the domestic mother lode of crude oil, Prudhoe Bay and other Alaskan North Slope oil wells have long been in decline. The production from these wells has slowed to the point where experts are looking at Alaska's Outer Continental Shelf (OCS) and the Arctic National Wildlife Refuge (ANWR), the largest protected wildlife refuge in the United States, located in Alaska's North Slope area.

Experts have estimated that 27 million barrels of currently recoverable oil lie beneath the seas off the Alaskan coast. That number will go up as oil-drilling technology improves and hard-to-recover oil becomes more accessible. Forecasters predict that the oil that companies can recover with today's technology and techniques would double the U.S. oil reserves. In an economy ravaged by fluctuating gas prices that affect every American consumer, the temptation to open up large swaths of the Arctic and Pacific oceans and other bodies of water surrounding Alaska is overwhelming.

Of course, many oppose expanding offshore oil exploration and development. The Alaskan fishing and tourist industries are major critics of more offshore drilling in Alaska, viewing expansion as a threat to their industries and jobs. Alaskan natives oppose offshore drilling because it will affect their way of life and relationship to the ocean. Environmentalists and scientists contest further development, charging that offshore oil wells pose a true and formidable threat to the delicate Alaskan ocean ecosystem, which harbors some distinctive and endangered creatures such as whales and polar bears.

The struggle between economic and environmental forces that characterizes the debate about offshore drilling nationwide is particularly vigorous in Alaska, a state that is thought to hold so much oil-producing potential. In addition to whether offshore drilling should be expanded in the United States, this chapter discusses offshore policies that the country should consider, such as reinstating the moratorium on new offshore drilling and expanding the "use it or lose it" laws to curb offshore oil development.

| *"Offshore development is a critical part of a comprehensive U.S. energy policy."*

Offshore Drilling in Alaska Should Be Expanded

Marvin E. Odum

Marvin E. Odum is the president of Shell Oil Company. In the following testimony in front of the Committee on Natural Resources, he asserts that to meet America's energy challenges, every potential source of energy must be explored. A big part of that, he argues, is making offshore drilling in Alaska more accessible for oil companies.

As you read, consider the following questions:

1. What does Marvin E. Odum perceive is the role of fossil fuels in America's energy future?

2. Does Odum believe in carte blanche offshore oil drilling?

3. How much money has Shell Oil Company paid for the rights to drill in the offshore region of Alaska, according to Odum?

Marvin E. Odum, "Offshore Drilling: Industrial Perspectives," Congressional Testimony: Oversight Hearing before the Committee on Natural Resources, February 25, 2009.

A comprehensive energy policy is critical to our economic recovery. As President [Barack] Obama said last night [February 24, 2009], we must invest in energy to reduce our dependence on foreign oil. I am hopeful that Congress and the administration will develop an energy and environment plan that addresses today's realities. Let me highlight just a few of those, as I see them.

First, I am concerned that our country has been lulled once again into complacency by the drop in the price of oil. Oil is now trading in the $30s, down from the $140 range that we saw just last summer [2008], but the energy challenge that dominated the headlines and gripped households has not vanished. It is simply hidden by the current economic slowdown.

When the economy recovers, the energy challenge will return, and I believe it will return with a vengeance. I urge Congress . . . to anticipate this and act now. Second, I am concerned that the debate will default to the same all-or-nothing choices—either alternative energy and conservation, or fossil fuels. Such a deadlock will not lead to forward progress.

U.S. Energy Policy Is in Transition

The facts are clear. Growing global demand dictates that all sources of energy and efficiency will be needed to fuel economic growth. Yes, policies are needed that will lead to the commercialization of green energy sources, but we must be realistic. The transition to this future will take time, even under the most optimistic circumstances.

This is not about a trade-off. It is about a transition, and the reality is that fossil fuels will be a major source of energy for the coming decades. The economic benefits of new oil and gas production simply cannot be overlooked, especially in the difficult circumstances that we face today. Producing more of our own energy will create jobs and fuel economic recovery. It will keep investment dollars here rather than exporting tril-

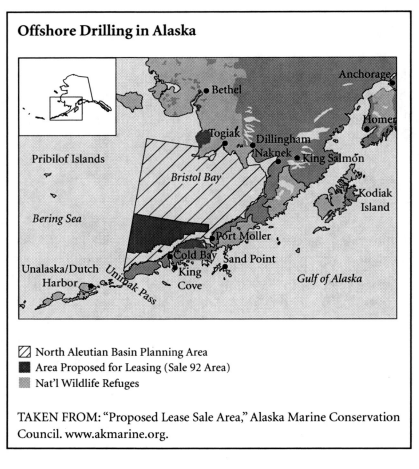

Offshore Drilling in Alaska

North Aleutian Basin Planning Area
Area Proposed for Leasing (Sale 92 Area)
Nat'l Wildlife Refuges

TAKEN FROM: "Proposed Lease Sale Area," Alaska Marine Conservation Council. www.akmarine.org.

lions of dollars to pay for imported oil. It will increase energy security, and it will generate significant new revenues for federal, state and local governments.

The Role of Offshore Drilling

Offshore development is a critical part of a comprehensive U.S. energy policy. Our nation should not return to a blanket moratorium. A moratorium, in my mind, is neither a strategy, nor a solution. Mr. Chairman [Congressman Nick J. Rahall], I do not support carte blanche offshore drilling. I agree with the need to address import issues, such as marine sanctuaries, "no go" areas, ecosystems and the management around those, states' rights and revenue sharing.

I welcome the opportunity to work with you and Secretary [Ken] Salazar on how these concepts can work, and how we best implement them. Access in the OCS [Outer Continental Shelf] is about more than just holding a lease sale. A case in point is Shell's experience in Alaska, where we are experiencing what I would call a de facto moratorium. I think this is important because it could be an indicator of what we may see as we open other areas for exploration and production.

Offshore Drilling in Alaska Has Enormous Potential

The Alaska OCS is open for leasing. The resource potential is enormous. Shell paid the federal Treasury over $2 billion for leases and has made additional investments, of course, to prepare for the exploration for oil and gas. Despite several years of effort, we have yet to be able to drill a single exploratory well.

We have learned firsthand several aspects of our regulatory and legal system need to be addressed as we look at opening new areas. The new administration, I know, is working for better government. In that spirit, what I am asking for is an efficient, well-resourced and coordinated regulatory process that functions in a timely manner.

Mr. Chairman, keeping 85 percent of our OCS off-limits while trillions of dollars to import our energy needs go offshore is not sound policy. We have the technology, we have the expertise, and the OCS can be explored and developed safely and responsibly to the great long-term benefit of this nation.

> "The threat of a major oil spill off
> Alaska's shores is growing rapidly as oil
> exploration and extraction expand into
> the Arctic."

Offshore Drilling in Alaska Should Be Limited

Margaret Williams

Margaret Williams is the managing director of World Wildlife Fund's (WWF's) Kamchatka/Bering Sea Ecoregion Program. In the following viewpoint, she underscores the environmental dangers of offshore oil drilling in Alaska. Williams strongly suggests that the Barack Obama administration turn back many of the George W. Bush administration policies in Alaska and slow down the pace of offshore drilling in the region for environmental reasons.

As you read, consider the following questions:

1. How big of an area of Alaska did the George W. Bush administration open up to offshore drilling, according to the author?

Margaret Williams, "Offshore Drilling in Alaska: Time to Slow the Rush," *Yale Environment 360*, November 17, 2008, p. Opinion. Copyright © 2008 Yale University. Reproduced by permission.

2. What unique forms of wildlife will be affected by off-shore drilling in Alaska?

3. What immediate step does the author believe the Barack Obama administration should take in Bristol Bay?

Now that the [2008] presidential campaign is over and gasoline has—for the time being—fallen well below $3 a gallon, the chants of "Drill, Baby, Drill!" have died down. That is a welcome development, for during the campaign voters were lured by the siren's song of offshore drilling and its supposed benefits, while hearing virtually nothing about its costs.

But the truth is that the environmental price of offshore drilling could be very high, and in no place more so than the state where I live: Alaska. And those of us who care deeply about Alaska's offshore waters—encompassing some of the cleanest and most biologically productive seas on earth—are hopeful that the [Barack] Obama administration and the new Congress will act decisively to reverse many decisions of the [former president George W.] Bush White House, which moved recklessly to drill off Alaska's coast, with little concern for the environment. Today, few Americans are aware that during the past eight years, the Bush administration has quietly opened a vast swath of offshore Alaska—an area more than twice the size of New York state—to drilling.

A Concerted Effort Is Needed to Protect Alaska

While some of the Bush administration's decisions can be un-done with the stroke of Barack Obama's pen, others cannot. A concerted effort must now be launched—in Congress, the Department of the Interior, and in the courts—to rein in the oil and gas leasing, exploration, and development that gathered significant momentum in the U.S. Arctic since 2000. The task is urgent not only because America's "Polar Bear Seas"—the Beaufort and Chukchi seas—and the salmon-rich waters of

Bristol Bay are home to an extraordinarily rich assemblage of fish, seabirds, whales, sea lions, and other marine mammals. That urgency is compounded because global warming is rapidly altering the marine environment. Regions now open to oil drilling are losing their sea ice, which is very bad news for the creatures, such as polar bears and ringed seals that depend on that ice to survive, though probably good news for those who would turn this pristine environment into the Saudi Arabia of the far North.

To slow down the offshore oil rush in Alaska, the new Obama administration should take the following steps.

First, as president, Obama should sign an executive order reversing the Bush administration's decision to drill on 5.6 million acres in Bristol Bay—home to what may be the greatest run of salmon on earth.

Second, President Obama's secretary of the interior must reform the department's Minerals Management Service (MMS), which oversees oil drilling. During the Bush administration, the MMS—plagued by corruption and sometimes staffed with former oil industry executives—has failed to ensure that proper environmental safeguards are in place before offshore drilling begins.

Third, under leases granted by the Bush administration, MMS has the right to suspend operations for environmental reasons. The Obama administration should invoke those rights until the oil industry demonstrates that it can operate in these extreme environments without risk to wildlife and marine resources. The new administration must prohibit drilling in environmentally sensitive areas, including prime polar bear habitat and whale migration routes.

Finally, working through the Department of the Interior and the Coast Guard, the Obama administration must vastly improve the ability of oil companies to respond to spills of heavy crude oil in Alaskan waters.

Government Has to Act

Conservation groups such as World Wildlife Fund (WWF)—where I am managing director of the Kamchatka/Bering Sea Ecoregion Program—are staunchly against drilling in biologically rich environments such as Bristol Bay. We also believe that any new offshore development in the Arctic should only be part of a transitional effort to a new energy policy. Before such drilling is considered, however, scientists must gather baseline biological data and quantify the cumulative impacts on the marine environment.

In recent years, the troubled Minerals Management Service has moved to develop offshore Alaska with an alacrity rarely seen in a federal agency. In the past year alone, the MMS has expanded the territory available for leasing in Alaska's offshore waters from roughly 10 million acres to more than 80 million. Earlier this year, MMS leased 2.9 million acres of that newly opened territory to oil companies in the remote Chukchi Sea. In addition, another 25 million acres of state and federal lands in the U.S. Arctic—onshore and off—are open to oil and gas leasing; of that, 13.5 million acres have already been leased. The only area that now remains totally off-limits to oil drilling is the coastal plain of the Arctic National Wildlife Refuge [ANWR].

Environmental Dangers Are Real

What's the worry? Comforted by massive oil industry advertising campaigns paid for with record profits, the average American could not be blamed for believing that the oil companies can drill oil on land and sea and transport it without a drop being spilled. Nothing could be farther from the truth. The threat of a major oil spill off Alaska's shores is growing rapidly as oil exploration and extraction expand into the Arctic.

Those of us who work regularly on these issues are alarmed for two principal reasons. First, state and federal environmental oversight of the oil industry in the Arctic has been abhorrent. And second, engineers and other experts widely agree that the technology to contain oil spills in sea ice environments simply doesn't exist.

Experts point to a yawning gap in "oil spill response" capacities between Arctic and temperate zones. If oil is spilled in the Arctic, we should expect it to stay there. We know all too well the impact of spilled oil on bird life and marine mammals, including polar bears: They die. MMS itself has said that the likelihood of a major oil spill in the Chukchi Sea is somewhere between 30 and 50 percent. Yet, most experts contend that it is exceedingly difficult, if not impossible, to use booms and other conventional technology to soak up heavy crude oil in waters covered in icebergs and sea ice.

Oil Companies Cause Environmental Problems

The *Exxon Valdez* disaster [on March 24, 1989], the worst oil spill in U.S. history, did catalyze improvements in the industry. But industry problems have persisted in the Arctic, including slipshod maintenance of key parts of the Trans-Alaska Pipeline and North Slope oil facilities.

On Prudhoe Bay, a lack of maintenance has caused major oil spills, leading to previous court injunctions against offshore exploration. British Petroleum [BP] went years without maintaining one of its North Slope pipelines, resulting in a spill of 200,000 gallons of oil in 2006 and a 3-day shutdown of BP's operations.

At sea, Shell Oil has aggressively pursued plans to develop offshore oil deposits. But Shell's exploration activity in the Beaufort Sea was halted when the U.S. Court of Appeals for the Ninth Circuit ruled that seismic testing would harm noise-sensitive bowhead whales and the indigenous communities that harvest them. The village of Point Hope, Alaska, joined by numerous native and environmental groups, is now challenging offshore development on the 2.9 million acres in the Chukchi Sea, contending that MMS violated federal environmental laws when it conducted the lease sales.

What President Obama Should Do

A top priority of the Obama administration must be to put an end to a culture at MMS in which science has routinely been quashed and corruption has been rampant. MMS has repeatedly demonstrated its allegiance to the oil industry, and there is a revolving door between the MMS and the industry as they trade senior staff back and forth. A senior MMS official retired from his agency post, only to turn up on the Shell payroll. The Interior Department's Alaska representative made a similar move to Shell Oil. But this cozy friendship is not unique to Alaska. This fall, the Interior Department's inspector general released details of an investigation demonstrating a history of oil companies bribing MMS employees with gifts and sexual favors.

Understandably, consumers throughout the United States are worried about the deepening economic crisis and the high cost of living. But the implication that drilling in the United States' marine environments will do much to help the average American is wrong. In fact, experts of all political persuasions acknowledge that even if offshore drilling were to begin today, a decade would pass before the oil could flow to the gas pumps. And even then, we'd only be paying a few cents less for each gallon of gas.

United States Needs a Comprehensive Energy Policy

President-Elect Obama must quash the myth of drilling our way to energy independence and develop a comprehensive energy policy that recognizes the benefits of conservation and efficiency and the necessity of moving to a low-carbon economy. In addition to slowing the rush to drill in Alaskan waters until comprehensive scientific studies are conducted, the new administration should consider buying back some or all of the $2.6 billion in leases sold last February [2008] on the Chukchi Sea. A precedent exists for such action: Following the *Exxon Valdez* spill, the federal government paid $90 million to repurchase leases in Bristol Bay.

Let's hope that as our new president and Congress develop an energy and climate policy, they will reject the vision of Arctic seas bristling with oil derricks and instead pursue a forward-looking plan that will both wean the United States off its addiction to oil and secure a future for the unique ecosystems and people of the Arctic.

"*The offshore moratorium is needed to protect our oceans and serve as a bridge to a clean energy economy.*"

Moratorium on Offshore Drilling Should Be Reinstated

Oceana

Oceana is an international organization devoted to fighting for the world's oceans and marine life. In the following viewpoint, Oceana joins with a number of other conservation groups to call for the Barack Obama administration to implement a rational policy to protect our oceans and coastlines from the environmental damage caused by offshore drilling. One of the main priorities, they argue, is reestablishing the moratorium on offshore drilling on the Outer Continental Shelf (OCS).

As you read, consider the following questions:

1. According to a 2003 Natural Resources Defense Council (NRDC) study, how many millions of gallons of oil end up in the world's oceans because of offshore drilling?

2. Why does Oceana believe that offshore drilling is especially dangerous in the Arctic?

Oceana, "Offshore Drilling Is Not the Answer," Oceana.org, January 15, 2009. Reproduced by permission.

3. How will the moratorium help protect the oceans?

Conservation organizations called on President-Elect [Barack] Obama and the 111th United States Congress today [January 15, 2009] to act quickly to set up a rational policy to protect our oceans, coasts—and planet—from the impacts of offshore oil and gas drilling. Specifically, in the first 100 days the new administration and Congress should take the following essential steps to set America on course toward a new energy economy:

- Reinstate the moratoria on offshore drilling in U.S waters on the Outer Continental Shelf [OCS] including sensitive ecosystems such as Bristol Bay, Alaska, while also providing for the National Academy of Sciences to assess current environmental baseline information and the impacts of leasing, exploration and development on ocean ecosystems.

- Begin the development of a comprehensive conservation and energy plan for the Arctic that provides a bridge from oil to renewable energy and conservation. The plan should include a comprehensive scientific assessment of the health, biodiversity and functioning of Arctic ecosystems, as well as the benefits and consequences of specific industrial activities. A precautionary, science-based approach must be applied to all oil and gas leasing, exploration and development activities in Arctic waters to determine if those activities should be conducted and if so, when, where and how.

Oil Drilling Poses Major Long-Term Risks to Sensitive Ocean Ecosystems

Offshore drilling creates a myriad of risks to the marine environment. According to the National Academy of Sciences, "No current cleanup methods remove more than a small fraction of oil spilled in marine waters, especially in the presence of broken ice." According to a 2003 Natural Resources Defense Council [NRDC] study, each year some 55 million gallons of oil—more than the amount spilled by the *Exxon Valdez*—is added to the world's oceans from offshore oil production, including both spills and operational discharges.

The Arctic Is Especially at Risk from Industrialization

Oil and gas activities pose particular threats to Arctic marine ecosystems and the people who use and depend on them. Wells, pipelines and vessels create a substantial risk of an oil spill. There is no proven method to clean up an oil spill in icy Arctic conditions, and such a spill would have catastrophic effects on important habitat for polar bears, other marine mammals, fish and recreational, spiritual and subsistence uses. In addition, the drill rigs, icebreakers, and seismic vessels necessary for oil and gas activities create substantial noise, which can cause bowhead whales to stray far from their normal migration routes and feeding grounds, impact the animals' hearing and potentially cause other problems. The negative effects incurred by the bowhead whales from these activities are also acutely felt by the native communities that depend upon them.

Expanded Oil Production Will Worsen Climate Change

Further production and use of oil runs directly counter to the approach needed to protect ocean ecosystems, low-lying coastal areas, coral reefs and the sensitive Arctic ecosystem from the devastating impacts of climate change. America needs to move away from fossil fuel–based energy toward renewable energy sources if we are to have any hope of reducing the harm caused by climate change.

We Need to End Our Dependence on Oil!

We must move toward a future with affordable, carbon-free energy, a healthy environment and freedom from the control

Reinstate the Moratorium on Offshore Drilling

For too long, we have reaped the fullness of the oceans' bounty. This bounty, however, is neither inexhaustible nor unlimited and we cannot expect to take forever without giving back. I urge you to move to reinstate the moratorium on drilling lease expansion. I further urge you to consider any resource exploitation activities conducted in the oceans over the Outer Continental Shelf [OCS] as conditional on both the merits of good planning and the establishment of an ocean trust fund and reinvestment in it.

Sam Farr, "Offshore Drilling: State Perspectives,"
Oversight Hearing before the Committee on Natural Resources,
U.S. House of Representatives, February 24, 2009.

of big oil companies. Part of this effort must include an emphasis on development of carbon-free technologies, including wind and solar power. Part of this effort must also be to provide lasting incentives for Americans to conserve energy.

Offshore Drilling Provides No Real Relief from High Gasoline Prices and Will Not Create Energy Independence

As the recent drop in oil prices demonstrates, global demand for oil drives the global price for oil. The market for oil is truly global—oil from the United States is sold all over the world and increased demand from countries like China and India is what will really affect the price of oil. Furthermore, the U.S. Energy Information Administration [EIA] has found that at peak production in 2025, increased drilling offshore would produce 220,000 barrels a day, which would account for less than 1 percent of current energy demand in the United States.

The Offshore Moratorium Is Needed to Protect Our Oceans and Serve as a Bridge to a Clean Energy Economy

In 1990, responding to the 11 million gallon *Exxon Valdez* oil spill, president George H.W. Bush used his executive authority to place a moratorium on any leasing or pre-leasing activity in Lower 48 offshore areas, including a small portion of the Eastern Gulf of Mexico. President [Bill] Clinton limited new drilling in the rich Bristol Bay fishing grounds in Alaska until 2012. In addition, since 1982, Congress has protected those same offshore waters with a moratorium emplaced as part of its appropriations process. Unfortunately, the congressional moratorium expired in 2008, and the executive moratorium was lifted by president George [W.] Bush. Reinstating both moratoria, including valuable habitat areas that were previously removed, such as Bristol Bay, must be a top priority in the first 100 days, as they will protect sensitive ocean and coastal areas and help stop climate change by reducing our use of fossil fuels. Because these moratoria do not include most of the offshore areas in Alaska, those areas should be part of a comprehensive conservation and energy plan for the Arctic that provides a bridge from oil to renewable energy and conservation.

> "The [Barack] Obama administration should continue with this important effort to expand domestic production of oil and gas."

Moratorium on Offshore Drilling Should Not Be Reinstated

Ben Lieberman

Ben Lieberman is senior policy analyst in energy and the environment in the Thomas A. Roe Institute for Economic Policy Studies at The Heritage Foundation. In the following viewpoint, he maintains that rescinding the moratorium on offshore drilling by the George W. Bush administration was smart energy policy. Lieberman contends continuing Bush's policy would be beneficial for the Barack Obama administration.

As you read, consider the following questions:

1. How much of America's territorial waters were closed to offshore drilling before the moratorium was lifted, according to the author?

Ben Lieberman, "Expanded Offshore Drilling Should Be a Part of U.S. Energy Policy," Heritage Foundation, Web Memo # 2284, February 10, 2009. Copyright © 2009 The Heritage Foundation. Reproduced by permission.

2. What does the author believe prompted the George W. Bush administration and public opinion to support rescinding the moratorium?

3. What does the author cite as a benefit of lifting the moratorium on offshore drilling?

L ast July [2008], President [George W.] Bush rescinded the long-standing executive moratorium on offshore drilling for oil and natural gas, and Congress followed suit by allowing its own restrictions to lapse on October 1 [2008]. Now, the Department of the Interior (DOI), which handles offshore energy leasing, has taken the first step toward making this energy available by publishing its proposal for a five-year leasing plan for 2010–2015. The [Barack] Obama administration should continue with this important effort to expand domestic production of oil and gas.

Background on U.S. Offshore Drilling

For many years, 85 percent of America's territorial waters— including most of the Pacific, Atlantic, and eastern Gulf of Mexico—were off limits to oil and natural gas exploration and drilling. The United States is the only nation in the world that has restricted its own energy supply to such an extent. An estimated 19 billion barrels of oil—nearly 30 years of current imports from Saudi Arabia—as well as substantial natural gas reserves are estimated to lie beneath these restricted areas. And it should be noted that these initial estimates tend to be on the low side.

Most of these restrictions were put in place at the behest of environmentalists and other drilling opponents in the late 1980s and 1990s, a time when gasoline was cheap and the need for additional supplies was not seen as great. But they have remained in place in recent years, even as gasoline hit $2.00 and then $3.00 a gallon, and even though state-of-the-art drilling technology has amassed a proven record of reducing the environmental impacts and risk of spills.

However, when prices hit $4.00 a gallon last summer, a fed-up public clamored for action, and polls showed more than 2 to 1 support for offshore drilling. The president and Congress finally listened and belatedly removed the legal restrictions. The next step in the process is for DOI's Minerals Management Service (MMS) to offer these areas for lease. MMS took this step on January 16 [2009], when it announced its 2010–2015 Draft Proposed Program and published it on January 21 [2009].

A Pro-Energy Opportunity for the Obama Administration

Though this proposal was crafted by the outgoing Bush administration, the Obama administration would do well to continue with it. It sets out a sensible plan for moving expeditiously but not recklessly toward leasing new areas, including some in the Pacific, Atlantic, offshore Alaska, and the Gulf of Mexico.

Unfortunately, some in Congress have suggested that they may reimpose all or part of the moratorium, and past statements suggest that President Obama may want to do the same. Further, even without a change in the law, new Secretary of the Interior Ken Salazar has the discretion to issue just a relative handful of new leases or simply drag out the leasing process indefinitely. However, such restrictions or delays would be a mistake.

The days of $4.00 a gallon gas are gone for now, but this is no time for complacency. The only reason for the sharp drop in oil and pump prices is a decline in demand due to the recession. But recessions do not last forever. Unless this nation begins to take action to increase supplies, prices will go right back up as soon as the economy turns around and demand picks up. Further, the process by which energy companies ob-

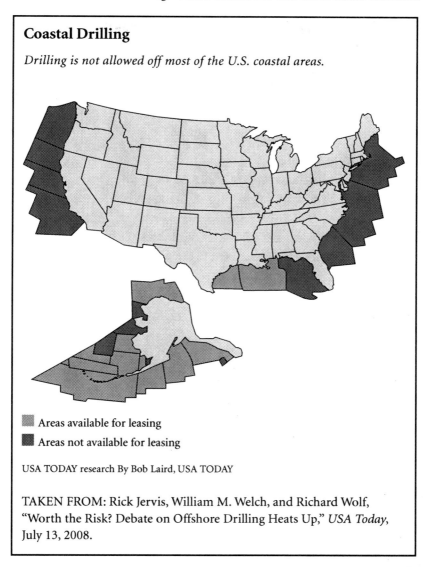

Coastal Drilling

Drilling is not allowed off most of the U.S. coastal areas.

▨ Areas available for leasing

■ Areas not available for leasing

USA TODAY research By Bob Laird, USA TODAY

TAKEN FROM: Rick Jervis, William M. Welch, and Richard Wolf, "Worth the Risk? Debate on Offshore Drilling Heats Up," *USA Today*, July 13, 2008.

tain a lease, explore for oil and gas, and then produce it takes a number of years to unfold, so the time to start the process is now.

Expanded offshore drilling would also create jobs, and unlike the taxpayer-funded jobs in the proposed [economic] stimulus package, the jobs created by a reinvigorated domestic energy industry would be well paying and long term and funded entirely by the private sector. And since the extra energy produced would help bring down future oil and natural gas prices, it would truly be a win-win for both producers and consumers.

Where to Go from Here

The comment period for the proposal lasts 60 days, after which DOI will move to the next steps, which involve a formal proposal by mid-summer and a final leasing program by as early as spring 2010. It would benefit all Americans if these steps lead expeditiously toward substantially expanded domestic offshore energy production in the years ahead.

> *"We don't need a 'use it or lose it' law—or more cheap-rhetoric, big-oil conspiracies."*

"Use It or Lose It" Laws Should Be Eliminated

Newt Gingrich and Roy Innis

Newt Gingrich is a senior fellow at the American Enterprise Institute for Public Policy Research (AEI). Roy Innis is chairman of the Congress of Racial Equality (CORE). In the following viewpoint, Gingrich and Innis insist that "use it or lose it" laws are counterproductive and not useful when it comes to oil exploration and drilling. Because finding oil is such a long, expensive, and cumbersome process susceptible to a number of obstacles, they argue that such laws will discourage offshore oil exploration and result in higher gas prices in the long run.

As you read, consider the following questions:

1. How long do oil companies have to act on oil leases they have purchased before they lose all rights to the land under the proposed law?

2. How much does a single offshore exploratory well cost, according to the authors?

Newt Gingrich and Roy Innis, "Idle Leases—or Addled Minds?" *Washington Times*, August 13, 2008. Reproduced by permission.

3. How many offshore oil wells out of every five do the authors say are successful?

Sen. Jeff Bingaman, Rep. Nick Rahall, House Speaker Nancy Pelosi and other members of Congress who oppose producing more American oil are in a bind.

They know voters are hurting from high gas prices and overwhelmingly want the government to allow more American oil production. But they can't side with the American people and risk upsetting their left-wing base. So they needed a way to make us think they support more drilling—while effectively preventing us from ever drilling a single new well.

"Use It or Lose It" Law

They think they've found a solution: a proposed "use it or lose it" law on federal leases for energy exploration. Messrs. Bingaman, Rahall and fellow drilling opponents accuse the oil industry of "sitting on" 68 million acres of "nonproducing" leased land. They want to force energy companies to "use" this leased land within 10 years—or lose all exploration and drilling rights.

America can only hope the proposed law is Mr. Bingaman and Mr. Rahall's clumsy attempt at political jujitsu. The alternative is that the politicians in charge of committees that determine U.S. energy policy are confused and ludicrously disconnected from reality.

First, lease agreements already require timely use of leased land. The 1992 Comprehensive [National] Energy Policy Act requires energy companies to comply with lease provisions, and explore expeditiously, or risk forfeiture of the lease. So the Bingaman-Rahall "solution" effectively duplicates current law.

Second, and more disturbingly, Mr. Bingaman and Mr. Rahall's groundless accusation and proposed legislation rely on the absurd assumption that every acre of land leased by the government contains oil. Obviously, that's not the case.

Finding Oil Is a Cumbersome and Expensive Process

The truth is, finding oil is a long, complex, cumbersome, expensive process. It starts with an idea—about what kinds of geologic structures are likely to hold this vital resource. Based on that idea, companies purchase leases: agreements that allow them to test their ideas, and hopefully find and produce oil and gas from leased properties.

Then geologists look at existing data and conduct seismic, magnetic and geophysical tests of the leased areas. They create detailed 3-D computer models of what subsurface rock formations look like, and whether there might be any "traps" that could hold petroleum.

Most of the time, all this painstaking, expensive initial analysis concludes that the likelihood is too small to justify drilling an exploratory well, since the cost of a single well can run $1 million to $5 million onshore, and $25 million to $100 million in deep offshore waters. Only 1 in 3 onshore wells finds enough oil or gas to produce profitably; in deep water, only 1 in 5 wells is commercial. Thus, only a small percentage of the leased acres ends up producing oil.

This is important because it means most of those 68 million acres Messrs. Bingaman and Rahall want to force oil companies to drill actually don't have enough oil to make it worth drilling. Either they know that, and are trying to deceive us; or they don't know it, because they haven't done their homework.

More Expenses in Process

Third, if a commercial discovery is made, more wells must be drilled to delineate the shape and extent of the deposit. Production facilities and pipelines must be designed, built, brought to the site and installed. Only after oil or gas is actually flowing does the lease become "producing."

A Pervasive Myth About Offshore Drilling

MYTH: Oil companies are sitting on 68 million acres of federal lands without drilling for oil or gas on any of it.

FACT: This false claim has become one of the Democrats' top talking points, but they can't back it up with any facts. Energy companies already are actively exploring their currently leased lands to find oil or gas. Once they determine that oil or gas is present, only then can they actually begin drilling. The entire process can take years.

John Boehner,
"FACT CHECK: 'Use It or Lose It'
Already the Law of the Land," 2008.
www.johnboehner.house.gov.

In one example, Shell Oil and its partners leased an area in 7,800 feet of water 200 miles off the Texas coast. They spent five years exploring and evaluating the area, punched several "dry holes," and finally drilled a discovery well in 2002. Three appraisal wells (at $100 million apiece) confirmed a major field, and in 2006 the company ordered a huge floating platform and pipeline system that will initiate production in 2010. Total investment: more than $3 billion.

That's hardly "sitting on their leases." But those leases will be "nonproducing" until 2010. Clearly, a "use it or lose it" law will not change these hard realities.

Further complications often stymie energy companies from obtaining and using leased land. Every step in the process must be preceded by environmental studies, oil spill response plans, onsite inspections, and permits. The process takes years, and every step is subject to delays, challenges—and litigation.

Environmental Concerns Cause Further Expense and Delays

In the Rocky Mountains, protests against lease sales rose from 27 percent of all leases in 2001 to 81 percent in 2007, according to government and industry records. Numerous additional prospects were never even offered, because land managers feared protests.

The justification used to be endangered species. Now it's climate change—as though U.S. oil causes global warming, but imported oil substitutes do not.

Where leases are issued, seismic and drilling work is often protested. Some years ago, an endangered plant held up drilling—until companies realized the Astragalus was locoweed, which ranchers had been trying to eradicate because it sickens cattle. This year, the excuses are drilling fluids that are 98 percent water and clay—and sage grouse, even though hunters shoot thousands of them every year.

The obstructionist tactics mean hundreds of millions of dollars in lease bonuses and rentals, seismic surveys and other exploration work are in limbo. None of this money was refunded to companies, and no interest is paid to the companies. The money would pay for thousands of wells that drilling opponents say companies refuse to drill.

These lands are nonproducing not because companies are procrastinating but because politicians and bureaucrats have bowed to pressure from radical environmentalists, and refused to issue permits.

Law Is Not Needed

We don't need a "use it or lose it" law—or more cheap-rhetoric, big-oil conspiracies. Congress simply needs to allow drilling on the 60 percent of onshore federal oil and gas prospects and 85 percent of Outer Continental Shelf prospects that it has placed off-limits.

Furthermore, instead of a "drill it or lose it" law, we need a "permit or pay" rule:

- When the government sits on permit applications for more than six months, companies no longer have to pay lease rents. Instead, they get interest on their bonus payments and expenses to date, and lease terms are extended.

- When environmental groups lose their legal actions, they pay the companies for the court costs, delays and attorney fees.

When you go to the ballot box this fall [2008], remember who is really behind the outrageous prices you're paying for the energy that makes your job, home, car and living standards possible. Remember the simple solution: Issue leases and permits. Drill here. Drill now. Pay less.

"Coal companies already comply with
requirements that they diligently develop federally leased lands—why
should oil companies be given special
treatment?"

"Use It or Lose It" Laws Should Be Tightened

Russ Feingold

*Russ Feingold is a U.S. senator representing Wisconsin. In the
following viewpoint, Feingold states that to spur oil exploration
and production in offshore areas already leased by oil companies,
he is proposing a "use it or lose it" law that requires oil companies to begin exploration on leased land within ten years or they
will lose all rights to it. Feingold maintains that only when they
can show they have been active on current leases can they receive
new leases on other land.*

As you read, consider the following questions:

1. How many millions of acres have been leased by oil
   companies but not developed, according to Russ Feingold?

Russ Feingold, "'Use It or Lose It' Spurs Oil Companies to Address Gas Prices," Fein
gold.senate.gov, August 12, 2008.

2. By what percentage does Feingold say the federal government has increased the number of drilling permits on public land from 1999 to 2007?

3. According to Feingold, how many unused permits are the oil companies sitting on and not using?

At the listening sessions I hold in every county of the state each year, Wisconsinites are rightly demanding action to lower the soaring oil prices that are devastating consumers at the pump and sending a rippling effect through our entire economy.

In the long term, we have to aggressively pursue alternative fuels, renewable energy, and energy efficiency to solve the energy crisis. But there are also some things we can do in the short term to help the many Wisconsinites who are struggling to provide for their day-to-day needs because of high gas prices.

"Use It or Lose It" Law

For starters, one of the quickest ways to increase oil production is by focusing on lands already under lease by oil companies. Oil companies collectively are not producing on about three-quarters of the federal lands and waters they have under lease. That's 68 million acres of lands and water that could potentially be producing oil, where leases have already been issued and miles and miles of pipeline and other infrastructure are already in place.

To help spur oil development on these lands, I introduced "use it or lose it" legislation requiring oil companies to show they are either producing oil or gas on current leases, or making progress on exploring and developing those leases, before they obtain more federal leases.

Coal companies already comply with requirements that they diligently develop federally leased lands—why should oil companies be given special treatment? My bill would create

Unused Oil Leases

Of the 90 million offshore acres the [oil] industry has leases to, mostly in the Gulf of Mexico, it is estimated that upwards of 70 million are not producing oil, according to both Democrats and oil industry sources.

Steve Hargreaves, "America's Untapped Oil,"
CNNMoney.com, June 28, 2008. http://money.cnn.com.

industry-wide accountability standards, which many of the oil companies say they are already capable of meeting.

Oil Companies Are Sitting on Oil

Oil companies continue to ask for more federal lands when they aren't producing oil on most of their current leases. The federal government has supported drilling on these lands in recent years by increasing the number of drilling permits for public lands by 361 percent from 1999 to 2007. As a result, oil companies now sit on nearly 10,000 unused permits from the Bureau of Land Management that they could use immediately to drill.

This failure to produce oil is even more surprising given that an oil executive told me at a recent Senate Judiciary Committee hearing that they have the manpower and infrastructure to put all their existing leases of federal lands into oil production.

U.S. Government Must Act

I support responsible efforts to increase domestic production. But in the long term, the solution to our energy crisis is to end what the president [George W. Bush] has called our addiction to oil. The president's own Energy Information Administration [EIA] has found that even if we open up all off-shore areas currently off-limits, there would be an insignificant effect on oil prices. We're already the third biggest producer of oil in the world, but with only two percent of the world's oil reserves, we simply cannot drill ourselves out of the problem.

We must diversify our energy portfolio—particularly in the transportation sector where 70 percent of oil is used. We need a real investment in alternative fuels and renewable energies and an emphasis on conservation and efficiency. Wisconsin has been a national leader in these areas, and that's something that can boost our economy in the long run by providing green jobs and energy security. I will continue to push on all fronts for policies that address high gas prices and move us toward renewable energy sources.

Periodical Bibliography

The following articles have been selected to supplement the diverse views presented in this chapter.

Joel Alicea — "Drilling in Silence," *National Review Online*, August 7, 2008. www.nationalreview.com.

Eric Alterman and George Zornick — "Think Again: Drilling Deep to Mislead on Oil Prices," Center for American Progress, June 26, 2008. www.americanprogress.org.

Michael Barone — "Common Cents," *National Review Online*, July 26, 2008. www.nationalreview.com.

Center for American Progress — "Ten Reasons Not to Lift the Offshore Drilling Moratorium," June 19, 2008. www.american progress.org.

Peter Dizikes — "Did You Hear That Alaska Has More Oil than the Middle East?" Salon.com, August 18, 2008. www.salon.com.

Kenneth P. Green and Abigail Haddad — "Incoherent at Best," American Enterprise Institute for Public Policy Research, September 2008. www.aei.org.

Robert W. Hahn — "A Strong Signal on Global Warming," Room for Debate Blog, January 26, 2009. http://room fordebate.blogs.nytimes.com.

Amy Myers Jaffe — "The Cowardly Giants," *Newsweek*, November 26, 2007.

Joseph Lawler — "Pumped and Primed," *American Spectator*, September 9, 2008.

OPPOSING
VIEWPOINTS®
SERIES

CHAPTER 4

What Other Energy Policies Should the U.S. Government Consider?

Chapter Preface

In the ongoing U.S. debate about energy and the country's dependence on oil, fuel economy is a subject that continues to generate passionate discussion among politicians, environmentalists, and energy industry experts. Defined as the average mileage traveled by an automobile per gallon of gasoline, fuel economy ratings are assigned to every automobile and truck sold in America. Experts concur that having a high fuel economy rating is a worthy goal for every car and truck on the road today: Because a car can travel more miles on a gallon of gas, a car owner buys less gas. With increasing numbers of fuel-efficient automobiles and trucks on the road, commentators assert that fuel prices will decrease and the country as a whole will have to import less crude oil and gasoline.

To facilitate the improvement of fuel efficiency standards, the U.S. government enacted the Corporate Average Fuel Economy (CAFE) regulations in 1975. These federal regulations aimed to improve the average fuel economy of cars and light trucks, including trucks, vans, and sport-utility vehicles (SUVs), by setting a minimum CAFE standard rating. The CAFE standard is the average annual fuel efficiency for a manufacturer's entire fleet. When setting CAFE ratings, Congress considers four key factors: 1) the technological possibility of setting the standard at a certain level; 2) the economic feasibility of setting the standard at a certain level; 3) the effects of other standards on fuel economy; and 4) the need of the country to conserve energy. Once set by Congress, the National Highway Traffic Safety Administration (NHTSA) regulates CAFE standards and the Environmental Protection Agency (EPA) measures fuel efficiency. If the average fuel economy of a car manufacturer's annual fleet of cars or trucks falls below the prescribed CAFE rating, the car company will be fined.

In 1978, when the government first began setting fuel economy standards, it calculated that light passenger vehicles should have an average fuel economy rating of 18 miles per gallon (mpg). In 2010 the CAFE rating for passenger vehicles is set at 27.5 mpg, which will increase in 2011 to 30.2 mpg. Studies have shown that by raising the CAFE rating over the years, CAFE regulations have conserved a significant amount of gas and saved consumers money through the use of more fuel-efficient vehicles.

On December 19, 2007, President George W. Bush signed the Energy Independence and Security Act. This legislation aims to improve vehicle fuel economy by setting an ambitious goal: a CAFE rating of 35 mpg by 2020. If the United States could meet such a goal, it would result in an increase of the fuel economy standards by 40 percent and save the country billions of gallons of fuel. The 35 mpg goal is the first standard that has been set above CAFE standards since the regulations were created in 1975.

Yet there are many commentators who oppose raising CAFE standards. They argue that by making cars more fuel efficient, consumers pay less and end up driving more, thereby increasing automobile emissions. In addition, raising fuel efficiency standards will not decrease our dependence on domestic or foreign oil; America will still be dependent on oil, even if our vehicles are more efficiently using it. Finally, these critics believe that the government shouldn't be setting fuel economy standards—the free market should.

The debate over fuel economy standards is only one of the issues discussed in the following chapter, which explores what types of energy policies the United States should consider. Other viewpoints investigate the significance of the Law of the Sea Treaty (LOST) and articulate the need for a comprehensive U.S. energy policy.

"As new technologies are developed over time, a progressive tightening of standards seems to make sense, given that the downside costs to the economy are not that huge, while 20 years from now we may be very glad that serious measures were taken during the intervening years to reduce the dependency of the transport system on conventional fossil fuels."

Fuel Efficiency Standards Should Be Raised

Ian Parry

Ian Parry is a senior fellow at Resources for the Future (RFF), focusing on environmental transportation and public health policies. In the United States, fuel economy (or CO_2 per mile) standards form the centerpiece of efforts to reduce oil dependence and greenhouse gas emissions from the transportation sector. In the following viewpoint, Parry questions the extent to which these policies can be rationalized on cost-benefit grounds.

Ian Parry, "Should Automobile Fuel Economy Standards Be Increased?" *Resources for the Future Weekly Policy Commentary*, September 17, 2007. Copyright © 2007 Resources for the Future. All rights reserved. Reproduced by permission. www.rff.org.

As you read, consider the following questions:

1. According to Ian Parry, what are the fuel economy standards for new cars being raised to by 2016?

2. Fuel economy standards for new light trucks and minivans are being raised to what by 2016?

3. Passenger vehicles account for what percentage of CO_2 emissions in the United States, according to the author?

As a result of recent legislation, manufacturers in the United States will be required to meet CO_2 [carbon dioxide] emissions per mile regulations that will raise the average fuel economy of new cars to 39 miles per gallon by 2016, and the average fuel economy of new light trucks (minivans, sport utility vehicles, pickups) to 30 miles per gallon. (Previous standards were 27.5 miles per gallon for cars and 24 miles per gallon for light trucks). To many people, it seems obvious that fuel economy standards should be tightened to reduce CO_2 emissions and oil dependence. After all, passenger vehicles account for about 20 percent and 45 percent of US CO_2 emissions and oil use, respectively. However, before we can conclude whether or not tightening fuel economy standards is a good idea, an economic assessment of the benefits and costs is appropriate. To think about this, it is helpful to separate out the effect of tighter standards on gasoline use, vehicle miles of travel, and the costs of automobile manufacture.

Facts Behind the Debate

Higher fuel economy standards would reduce the demand for gasoline, thereby producing "externality" benefits (societal benefits that are not taken into account by individuals) in the form of avoided CO_2 emissions and reduced nationwide dependence on oil. Most estimates of economic damages from future global warming—agricultural impacts, rising sea levels and increased storm intensity, health effects from spreading tropical disease, and so on—are in the order of $20 per ton of current CO_2 emissions, or about 20 cents per gallon of gasoline (burning a gallon of gasoline produces nearly 0.01 tons of CO_2). Damages are much higher if, as advocated by some economists, more weight is given to the well-being of future generations or extreme climate risks.

The broader external costs of oil dependence include the risk of macroeconomic disruption costs from oil price shocks that might not be fully taken into account by the private sector, such as some costs associated with the temporary idling of labor and capital. And while the United States as a whole has an influence on the world oil market, individual oil importers do not consider the impact of their own infinitesimal consumption on increasing the world oil price, which imposes an external cost by increasing the amount of money transferred from other oil importers in the United States to foreign oil suppliers. Paul Leiby estimates that external costs from macroeconomic disruption risks and US market power amount to, very roughly, 30 cents per gallon of gasoline. Dependence on oil also constrains US foreign policy and possibly undermines national security. Politicians may be reluctant to challenge oil-producing countries on human rights and other issues, and oil revenues may help certain hostile governments, terrorists, and other unsavory groups. Putting an additional dollar figure on these broader foreign policy and national security costs is extremely difficult however.

Motorists already pay, at least in part, for the external costs of fuel consumption through federal and state gasoline taxes, which add about 40 cents per gallon to the price at the pump. According to basic tax theory, reducing gasoline use produces net benefits to society only to the extent that CO_2 and oil dependence externalities exceed fuel taxes. Our discussion suggests, albeit very tentatively, that external costs that have been quantified might largely offset by prevailing fuel taxes. However, accounting for national security and other

New Solutions to Oil Crunch

Fuel efficiency: Individuals can save money and cut oil consumption by driving more efficiently, and the government can provide incentives for doing so. Businesses can offer programs that reward employees for driving less.

Smarter cars: The auto industry can stop fighting higher fuel economy standards and invest in the transportation options of the future. The government can adopt clean-fuel requirements that drive the development of low-carbon alternatives.

Natural Resources Defense Council,
"Build the Clean Energy Economy,"
Move America Beyond Oil, 2009.
http://beyondoil.nrdc.org.

costs would seem to imply net benefits overall from reducing gasoline use, though the magnitude of the gain is very difficult to pin down.

Impact of Fuel Economy Standards on Oil Prices

Critics of fuel economy standards sometimes point to the perverse effect of higher fuel economy on lowering fuel costs per mile and increasing the incentive to drive, which can increase highway congestion, accidents, and pollution. However, according to a recent study by Kenneth [A.] Small and Kurt Van Dender, less than 10 percent of the fuel savings from better fuel economy are offset by increased driving. While the costs of this "rebound effect" should be factored into an assessment of fuel economy regulations, they are less important than other factors.

Binding fuel economy regulations induce auto manufacturers to incorporate more fuel-saving technologies into new vehicles, leading to higher vehicle production costs and prices. However, a number of studies, such as one in 2002 by the National Research Council, suggest that fuel-saving benefits over the vehicle life would outweigh the up-front installation costs for many emerging technologies. Some analysts argue that these apparent "win-win" technologies may not be adopted without tighter fuel economy regulations, however, because consumers may underappreciate the benefits of better fuel economy if they are preoccupied with other vehicle attributes like power, comfort, and safety. On the other hand, others argue that forcing technology adoption may be costly if consumers would instead prefer new technologies be used to improve other vehicle characteristics, such as increased horsepower, rather than fuel economy. Another possibility is that manufacturers may meet higher fuel economy requirements by reducing vehicle weight and size; this can raise injury risks for occupants of these vehicles, though it makes the roads a little safer for other drivers.

In short, the case for tightening fuel economy regulations can be argued either way, because it is difficult to judge precisely how manufacturers will respond, and how consumers will value changes in vehicle technology. But, most importantly, the climate and national security benefits from reduced gasoline use are much disputed. Another policy option is to raise fuel taxes, which unlike fuel economy regulations, would reduce congestion and other highway externalities, through reducing vehicle miles traveled. While the case for higher fuel taxes is more clear-cut, this option lacks political traction at present.

When I first began studying fuel economy regulations, the case for tightening the standards looked rather dubious to me. However, my perspective has changed somewhat as the difficulties in doing a nice, clean cost-benefit analysis have become more apparent. Moreover, colleagues of mine who have thought hard about the issue—like Carolyn Fischer, Lawrence Goulder, Winston Harrington, Richard Newell, William Pizer, Paul Portney, Philip Sharp, and Kenneth [A.] Small—are sympathetic to higher standards, if they are not ramped up too rapidly and reforms permit more trading of fuel economy credits to keep down program costs. My own view is that if the argument comes down to doing nothing or tightening fuel economy regulations, then the latter is what you do. As new technologies are developed over time, a progressive tightening of standards seems to make sense, given that the downside costs to the economy are not that huge, while 20 years from now we may be very glad that serious measures were taken during the intervening years to reduce the dependency of the transport system on conventional fossil fuels.

> *"There are no problems for CAFE [Cor-*
> *porate Average Fuel Economy] stan-*
> *dards to solve. Hence, they shouldn't be*
> *tightened; they should be repealed."*

Fuel Efficiency Standards Should Not Be Raised

Jerry Taylor and Peter Van Doren

Jerry Taylor and Peter Van Doren are senior fellows at the Cato Institute. In the following viewpoint, they argue that mandating energy conservation in the form of raising Corporate Average Fuel Economy (CAFE) standards will not work. They also suggest that there is no relationship between Islamic terrorism and the U.S. addiction to oil.

As you read, consider the following questions:

1. According to the authors, the U.S. Senate wants to mandate that every car, pickup truck, and sport-utility vehicle (SUV) sold in 2020 has a fuel efficiency of how many miles per gallon?

2. What do the authors cite is the fuel efficiency mandate right now?

Jerry Taylor and Peter Van Doren, "Don't Raise CAFE Standards," *National Review Online*, August 1, 2007. Copyright © 2007 by National Review, Inc., 215 Lexington Avenue, New York, NY 10016. Reproduced by permission.

3. Why do the authors believe that raising Corporate Average Fuel Economy (CAFE) standards won't decrease the amount of pollution coming from U.S. cars?

Everybody in Washington wants to force the auto industry to make more fuel-efficient cars and trucks. President [George W.] Bush wants to require new vehicles to meet federal standards (to be determined) based on how heavy they are. The Senate wants to mandate that every car, pickup truck, and SUV [sport-utility vehicle] sold in 2020 average a fuel efficiency of at least 35 miles per gallon [mpg]—far more aggressive than the 27.5 mile per gallon standard now in place for passenger vehicles. The House could offer an amendment on fuel standards from the floor on Friday [August 3, 2007]. Either way, we'll find out later this week what's in store.

Fuel Efficiency Is Overvalued

Would the market produce "too little" conservation without Corporate Average Fuel Economy (CAFE) standards? At first glance, no. The "right" (that is, efficient) amount of gasoline consumption will occur naturally as long as fuel markets are free and gasoline prices reflect total costs. In fact, a review of market data by Clemson University economist Molly Espey and Santosh Nair found that consumers actually *overvalue* fuel efficiency. That is, they pay more up front in higher car prices than the present value of the fuel savings over the lifetimes of the cars.

But driving imposes costs on others that aren't reflected in fuel prices, like environmental degradation. Because gasoline prices do not reflect total costs, consumption is higher than it ought to be. Congress is therefore doing the economy a favor by mandating increased increments of energy conservation, right?

The argument is clever, but wrong.

CAFE Standards Don't Work

In 1975, Congress reacted to the 1973 oil embargo imposed by the Organization of the Petroleum Exporting Countries (OPEC) by establishing the Corporate Average Fuel Economy (CAFE) program as part of the Energy Policy and Conservation Act [EPCA]. The goal of the program was to reduce U.S. dependence on imported oil and consumption of gasoline. Advocates also hoped it would improve air quality. But the evidence shows that it has failed to meet its goals; worse, it has had unintended consequences that increase the risk of injury to Americans. Instead of perpetuating such a program, Congress should consider repealing the CAFE standards and finding new market-based solutions to reduce high gasoline consumption and rising prices.

Charli E. Coon,
"Why the Government's CAFE Standards
for Fuel Efficiency Should be Repealed, Not Increased,"
The Heritage Foundation, July 11, 2001.

Raising CAFE Standards Is Ineffective

Increasing CAFE standards will not decrease the amount of pollution coming from the U.S. auto fleet. That's because we regulate emissions per mile traveled, not per gallon of gasoline burned. Improvements in fuel efficiency reduce the cost of driving and thus increase vehicle miles traveled. Moreover, automakers have an incentive to offset the costs associated with improving fuel efficiency by spending less complying with federal pollution standards with which they currently over-comply.

Those two observations explain calculations from Pennsylvania State [University] economist Andrew Kleit showing that a 50 percent increase in CAFE standards would increase total emissions of volatile organic compounds by 2.3 percent, nitrogen oxide emissions by 3.8 percent, and carbon monoxide emissions by 5 percent.

Fuel Standards and National Security

Another rationale for CAFE standards is that gasoline purchases send money to foreign terrorists who kill and maim with our dollars. Energy conservation, according to many, is our "ace in the hole" against al Qaeda and its ilk.

If there were a relationship between our "energy addiction" and Islamic terrorism, one would expect to find a correlation between world crude oil prices and Islamic terror attacks or mortality from the same. But there is no statistical relationship between the two. Terrorism is a very low-cost endeavor and manpower, not money, is its necessary determinant. That explains why even the lowest inflation-adjusted oil prices in history proved no obstacle to the rise of Islamic terror organizations in the 1990s.

While it's true that nasty regimes like Iran are getting rich off our driving habits, the extent to which oil profits fuel its nastiness is unclear. After all, Pakistan is a poor country with no oil revenues, but it had no problem building a nuclear arsenal. The same goes for North Korea. Iran without oil revenues might look like Syria. Venezuela without oil revenues might look like Cuba. In short, while rich bad actors are probably more dangerous than poor ones, oil revenues don't seem to make much difference at the margin.

Fuel Efficiency and Energy Independence

Finally, we're told that CAFE helps secure our energy independence. But the amount of oil we import is related to the difference between domestic and foreign crude oil prices. Reducing oil demand may reduce the total amount of oil we consume, but it will not reduce the degree to which we rely on foreign oil to meet our needs.

Regardless, tightening CAFE standards would have little impact on any of these alleged problems. If the Senate's proposed CAFE standard of 35 mpg by 2020 were to become law, it would reduce oil consumption by, at most, about 1.2 million barrels a day. Given that the Energy Information Administration [EIA] thinks world crude oil production would be 103.8 million barrels a day by 2020, the reduction would be 1.2 percent of global demand and result in a 1.3 percent decline in price; nowhere near enough to defund terrorists, denude oil producers of wealth, or secure energy independence.

Congress has no business dictating automotive fuel efficiency. That's a job for consumers, not vote-hustling politicians. There are no problems for CAFE standards to solve. Hence, they shouldn't be tightened; they should be repealed.

> "*[Ratifying the Law of the Sea Convention] would help protect U.S. national security, advance U.S. economic interests, and protect the marine environment.*"

Law of the Sea Treaty (LOST) Should Be Ratified

David B. Sandalow

David B. Sandalow is a senior fellow in foreign policy at the Brookings Institution. In the following viewpoint, he urges the United States to follow the recommendations of the U.S. Senate Committee on Foreign Relations and immediately ratify the Law of the Sea Convention (also known as the Law of the Sea Treaty, or LOST). Sandalow argues that the treaty is necessary to protect national security and for environmental reasons.

As you read, consider the following questions:

1. What are a few of the provisions of the Law of the Sea Convention?

2. When were Law of the Sea Convention's provisions originally accepted?

David B. Sandalow, "Law of the Sea Convention: Should the U.S. Join?" Brookings Policy Brief Series # 136, August, 2004. Copyright © 2004 Brookings Institution. Reproduced by permission.

3. How many countries are parties to the convention today?

The United States has vital interests in the oceans. U.S. national security depends on naval mobility. U.S. prosperity depends on underwater energy resources. Ocean fisheries help feed the United States and much of the world.

On February 25, 2004, the Senate Committee on Foreign Relations unanimously recommended that the United States accede to the Law of the Sea Convention [also known as Law of the Sea Treaty (LOST)], which sets forth a comprehensive framework of rules for governing the oceans. The recommendation followed two hearings in which the committee heard testimony supporting the convention from the [George W.] Bush administration, the armed services, ocean industries, and environmental groups, among others. Following the favorable report from [the Senate Committee on] Foreign Relations, other congressional committees held hearings at which several lawmakers raised concerns about the treaty.

The United States should promptly join the Law of the Sea Convention. Doing so would help protect U.S. national security, advance U.S. economic interests, and protect the marine environment. Prompt action is needed to ensure that the United States is a party by November 2004, when the convention is open to amendment for the first time.

Background on Law of the Sea Convention

The Convention on the Law of the Sea is sometimes called a "constitution" for the oceans. Among its many provisions, the convention limits coastal nations to a 12-mile territorial sea, establishes 200-mile exclusive economic zones, requires nations to work together to conserve high seas fisheries, and establishes a legal regime for the creation of property rights in minerals found beneath the deep ocean floor.

Historically, rules concerning use of the oceans were established by customary international law—a term used to describe practices considered legally required by most nations from time to time. The uncertainties inherent in such an approach led, in 1958, to the adoption of four conventions on oceans governance. The conventions were promptly ratified by the United States and many other countries, but soon came to be seen as insufficient. In particular, during the 1960s, the United States became increasingly concerned about the growing number of coastal states asserting control over vast reaches of the oceans. New issues—including marine pollution—gained greater prominence. In 1973, negotiations were launched for a comprehensive Convention on the Law of the Sea.

The convention was adopted in 1982. Its provisions reflected long-standing U.S. negotiating objectives, including recognition of navigational and overflight freedoms, limits on coastal state jurisdiction to a 12-mile territorial sea, the establishment of 200-mile exclusive economic zones, and rights to the ocean floor to the edge of the continental shelf. However, the agreement also contained provisions on deep seabed mining at odds with U.S. interests, including requirements for the mandatory transfer of technologies.

United States Supported Convention at One Time

President [Ronald] Reagan praised the convention's "many positive and very significant accomplishments," but declined to sign because of the deep seabed mining provisions. In March 1983, President Reagan issued an Ocean Policy Statement announcing the United States' intention to act generally in accordance with the terms of the convention.

Further negotiations over the convention's deep seabed mining provisions were launched in 1990. These talks concluded in 1994 with a new agreement on deep seabed mining that addressed all of the concerns that the Reagan administration had identified a decade earlier. Also in 1994, the convention entered into force after the sixtieth nation joined.

In October 1994, the convention was transmitted to the Senate for approval. Sen. Jesse Helms (R-N.C.), then chairman of the Senate Committee on Foreign Relations, declined to hold hearings. After Helms retired in January 2003, Sen. Richard Lugar (R-Ind.), the new chair of [the Senate Committee on] Foreign Relations, held two hearings on the treaty. On February 25, 2004, the Senate Committee on Foreign Relations unanimously recommended that the United States join the convention.

Today, more than 140 countries are parties to the Law of the Sea Convention.

National Security Considerations

U.S. military operations depend on naval mobility. By codifying navigational and overflight freedoms long asserted by the United States, the convention improves access rights in the oceans for our armed forces, reducing operational burdens and helping avert conflict.

Historically, the U.S. Navy was required to contend with widely varying and excessive claims by coastal nations concerning access to the oceans. In the 1940s, for example, Chile asserted the right to control access by all vessels within two hundred miles of its coast. Later, Indonesia asserted a similar right with regard to all waters between its many islands.

These claims and many others are effectively resolved by the convention, which recognizes navigational and overflight freedoms within 200-mile exclusive economic zones and through key international straits and archipelagoes. The convention also recognizes rights of passage through territorial seas, without notice and regardless of means of propulsion, as well as navigational and overflight freedoms on the high seas.

The results include less need for military assets to maintain maritime access rights and reduced risk of conflict.

Failure to Ratify Convention Risks Security

However, the failure of the United States to join the Law of the Sea Convention puts these gains at risk.

First, there is a risk that important provisions could be weakened by amendment, beginning in November 2004, when the treaty is open for amendment for the first time. Currently, for example, the convention prohibits coastal states from denying transit rights to a vessel based upon its means of propulsion. Some states, however, may propose to amend this provision to allow exclusion of nuclear-powered vessels. Under the convention, no amendment may be adopted unless the parties agree by consensus (or, if every effort to reach consensus failed, more than two-thirds of the parties present agree both on certain procedural matters and on the proposed amendment). As a party, the United States would have a much greater ability to defeat amendments that are not in the U.S. interest, by blocking consensus or voting against such amendments.

Second, by staying outside the convention, the United States increases the risk of backsliding by nations that have put aside excessive maritime claims from years past. Pressures from coastal states to expand their maritime jurisdiction will not disappear in the years ahead—indeed such pressures will likely grow. Incremental unraveling of many gains under the convention is more likely if the world's leading maritime power remains a nonparty.

Law of the Sea Convention Identified as a Top Security Priority

For these reasons and others, General Richard B. Myers, chairman of the Joint Chiefs of Staff, recently called ratification of the treaty by the United States "a top national security priority." Admiral Vern Clark, Chief of Naval Operations, reiterated the Navy's long-standing support for U.S. ratification, explaining that "by joining the convention, we further ensure the freedom to get to the fight, twenty-four hours a day and seven days a week, without a permission slip."

Some columnists and think tank analysts have argued that U.S. accession to the convention is unnecessary because excessive maritime claims can be addressed by invoking customary international law and with "operational assertions" by the U.S. military. But such an approach is less certain, more risky, and more costly than taking advantage of the convention. Customary law is by nature subject to varying interpretations and change over time. Operational assertions—sending military ships and aircraft into contested areas—involve risk to naval personnel as well as political costs. Such assertions should be conducted aggressively where needed, but avoided where possible.

In addition, some columnists and think tank analysts have argued that U.S. accession to the convention would interfere with the Proliferation Security Initiative (PSI), under which the United States and more than a dozen allies have agreed to interdict some ships that may present a nonproliferation risk. In fact, the convention expands the list of justifications for ship interdictions set forth in its predecessor, the 1958 Convention on the High Seas, to which the United States has been a party for more than forty years. Among the many legal bases that may be applicable to interdictions under the PSI are the jurisdiction of coastal states in their territorial seas, the right to board stateless vessels, an agreement concerning high-seas boarding with a flag state (the country of origin of an ocean-going vessel) and the inherent right of self-defense. Indeed several allies have recently expressed concern about the U.S. failure to ratify the convention, asserting that this failure could weaken the PSI.

Impact on U.S. Intelligence Capabilities

Finally, some treaty opponents have argued that joining the convention would hamper U.S. intelligence activities, citing a supposed restriction on intelligence-gathering and submerged transit of submarines in coastal waters. This argument is based on a simple misreading of Articles 19 and 20 of the convention, which impose no restrictions on any activity but simply establish conditions for invoking the "right of innocent passage."

As Admiral Clark has written, the convention "supports U.S. efforts in the war on terrorism by providing important stability and codifying navigational and overflight freedoms, while leaving unaffected intelligence collection activities."

Commercial Considerations

The U.S. economy depends on the oceans. Goods worth more than $700 billion are shipped through U.S. ports each year. More than a third of oil and gas produced around the world each year comes from offshore wells. (For U.S. oil and gas production, the figure is roughly 25 percent.) U.S. fisheries had landings in excess of $3 billion in 2002. Submarine cables are essential to global communications and therefore much of global commerce.

The Law of the Sea Convention helps promote U.S. commercial interests in several important respects.

First, the navigational freedoms recognized under the convention provide a stable environment for global commerce. Clear rules with widespread acceptance facilitate international trade and reduce risks to the many industries that depend upon marine transport.

Second, the U.S. oil and gas industry benefits from the convention's rules concerning offshore resources. Under the convention, coastal nations have exclusive authority over all resources within two hundred miles of shore. In addition, coastal nations have authority over the ocean floor beyond this 200-mile zone, to the edge of the continental shelf.

This latter provision is especially beneficial for the United States, which has the largest continental shelf in the world.

Vast areas of the ocean floor off Alaska, Maine, and other states are brought under U.S. jurisdiction as a result of this provision. With expected advances in deep water drilling technologies, these areas hold vast potential for oil and gas production.

Convention Good for Offshore Oil Drilling

In addition, the convention offers a ready set of procedures for delineating the outer limit of each country's continental shelf. These procedures help provide the certainty needed for major capital investment in offshore oil and gas facilities.

However, these procedures are only available to nations that join the convention. In addition, only nations that join the convention can nominate commissioners to the convention's Commission on the Limits of the Continental Shelf.

Currently pending before this commission is a submission by Russia concerning the Arctic Ocean. Based on preliminary analyses, the United States is concerned that Russia is claiming territory that fails to meet the convention's criteria for the continental shelf. Unless the United States promptly ratifies the convention, decisions concerning Russia's submission will be made without full U.S. influence or input. Claims are also being submitted by Australia and Brazil.

For these reasons and others, the American Petroleum Institute [API], the International Association of Drilling Contractors [IADC], and the National Ocean Industries Association [NOIA] all support U.S. ratification of the convention.

Revenue-Sharing Issues

Some opponents of ratification have objected to the convention's provisions concerning revenue sharing of proceeds from the outer continental shelf. Under the convention, no payments are owed for the first five years of production (which are typically the most productive). Beginning in year six, payments equal to 1 percent of the value of production at the site, increasing 1 percent each year to a maximum of 7 percent, are owed to the International Seabed Authority [ISA].

Significantly, the U.S. oil and gas industry, which would likely make these payments, does not oppose the convention's revenue-sharing provisions. After noting "the significant resource potential of the broad U.S. continental shelf," Rowan Companies, representing the American Petroleum Institute and other major industry groups, told the Senate Committee on Foreign Relations in October 2003 that "on balance the package contained in the convention, including the modest revenue-sharing provision, clearly serves U.S. interests."

Law of the Sea Convention and Ocean Fisheries

Finally, the convention promotes the United States' substantial commercial interests in ocean fisheries. The recognition of our 200-mile exclusive economic zone by other nations is fundamental to gaining full value from our rich fisheries. (Under the convention, the United States has the exclusive right to determine the allowable catch of living resources within this 200-mile zone.) The requirement that nations work together in managing migratory species is equally fundamental to maintaining the health of many fish stocks.

The U.S. fishing industry, including the U.S. Tuna Foundation, strongly supports U.S. ratification of the convention.

Environmental Considerations

The ocean environment is under enormous stress. Many fisheries are depleted or collapsing. Pollution plagues highly populated coastal regions. Nonnative species threaten ocean ecosystems around the globe.

The Law of the Sea Convention provides a comprehensive framework for international cooperation to protect the marine environment. It imposes minimum requirements—all of which are already being met by the United States—to protect and preserve the marine environment. Under the convention, states are required to take measures to address pollution from vessels and land-based sources, to prevent the introduction of alien or invasive species, and to conserve and manage coastal fisheries.

The convention also requires states to work together to protect the oceans. States are required to cooperate in the management of high seas fish stocks, as well as stocks that migrate between the high seas and exclusive economic zones, setting the stage for regional agreements essential to managing ocean fisheries. States are also required to work together to protect marine mammals, which are given special protections under the convention.

Convention Works to the Advantage of the United States

The standards for environmental protection set forth in the convention work strongly to the advantage of the United States, which has already met and in most cases significantly exceeded these standards but necessarily depends on actions by other nations to protect the marine environment.

The convention has strong support from environmental groups, including the National Environmental Trust, the Ocean Conservancy, and the World Wildlife Fund [WWF].

Some observers have expressed concern that the convention gives undue preference to navigational rights over the rights of coastal states to protect their shores from marine pollution. However, the convention affirms the sovereign right of all nations to impose conditions for port entry designed to protect the marine environment and recognizes numerous coastal state authorities to address polluting activities of foreign vessels. These and other provisions strike a reasonable balance between the United States' interests as a coastal state and seagoing nation.

185

What Does the United States Have in Common with Libya, Iran, Syria and North Korea?

All five countries have signed but failed to ratify the Convention on the Law of the Sea.

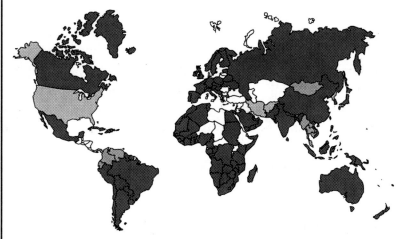

*The dark-colored countries have ratified, the grey countries have signed but not ratified, and the light-colored countries have not signed or ratified.

TAKEN FROM: *Law of the Sea Briefing Book*, 2008.

Deep Seabed Mining

For decades, engineers have explored ways to extract metals from the deep seabed. Deposits of manganese, cobalt, and methane hydrates have attracted particular interest. At present, however, there are no commercial deep seabed mining projects, largely because costs are much higher than for land-based mining. Cost is expected to remain a significant barrier to mining in the deep ocean for years to come.

Historically, the lack of clear property rights was also a barrier to development. The high seas and ocean floor beneath them have long been considered part of the global commons, beyond the reach of national jurisdiction. As such, it was unclear how nations or companies might establish legal title to minerals retrieved from the ocean floor. Investors were not expected to commit to the substantial funds needed for commercial development absent assurance that property rights would be widely recognized.

International Seabed Authority (ISA) Agreement

In 1994, more than 100 nations adopted a set of rules governing deep seabed mining. The 1994 agreement applies free market principles to deep seabed mining, establishing a mechanism for vesting title in minerals in the entity that recovers them from the ocean floor. The agreement establishes an International Seabed Authority (ISA) with responsibility for supervising this process. The ISA is an independent international organization—not a part of the United Nations. It is governed by a council (with principal executive authority) and an assembly (which gives final approval to regulations and budgets). As a party to the convention, the United States would be a permanent member of the council and have the ability, under relevant voting rules, to block most substantive decisions of the authority, including any decisions with financial or budgetary implications and any decisions to adopt rules, regulations, or procedures relating to the deep seabed mining regime.

The 1994 agreement also recognized the long-standing view that the deep ocean floor is part of the global commons and beyond the reach of national jurisdiction.

The agreement addresses in full all concerns identified by President Reagan a decade earlier. Technology transfer requirements—a principal objection in 1982—were deleted from the agreement.

The 1994 agreement is a legally binding modification of Part XI of the Law of the Sea Convention.

Convention Protects U.S. Mining Interests

Some opponents of U.S. ratification have expressed concern that American companies would be the victims of discrimination in mining approvals and that companies would owe substantial fees to the International Seabed Authority. However, U.S. voting rights on the council and assembly would prevent such results. Furthermore, failure by the United States to ratify operates as the most effective discrimination against U.S. companies. Few if any companies would invest the enormous sums needed for deep seabed mining without ISA approval, forcing U.S. companies to work through foreign governments in order to secure widely recognized property rights in minerals from the deep seabed.

Diverse Support

Diverse voices—including the Joint Chiefs of Staff, the Navy, the oil and gas industry, the fishing industry and major environmental groups—have expressed strong support for U.S. ratification of the Law of the Sea Convention. The U.S. Commission on Ocean Policy, appointed by President Bush pursuant to the Oceans Act of 2000, unanimously recommended U.S. ratification, as did the privately appointed Pew Oceans Commission. This breadth of support reflects the many benefits the United States would enjoy from ratifying the convention.

By its terms, the convention is open to amendment for the first time in November 2004—the tenth anniversary of its entry into force. At that time, many U.S. gains under the convention may be at risk.

In February 2002, the Bush administration declared that U.S. accession to the convention was "urgent." The Senate should promptly approve the Law of the Sea Convention to protect and promote wide-ranging U.S. interests. [Editor's note: As of October 2009, the U.S. Senate had not yet ratified the Law of the Sea Convention.]

> "The American people are rightfully de-
> manding solutions to our energy crisis,
> but make no mistake: LOST [Law of
> the Sea Treaty] is not one of them."

Law of the Sea Treaty (LOST) Should Not Be Ratified

Ben Lerner

*Ben Lerner is director of policy operations at the Center for Se-
curity Policy. In the following viewpoint, he asserts that contrary
to some reports, Law of the Sea Treaty (LOST), which is also
known as Law of the Sea Convention, will ultimately hurt the
oil industry and the American people by raising oil prices. Lerner
argues that LOST will also force American companies to share
technology with other countries and impose environmental regulations that will cost consumers money.*

As you read, consider the following questions:

1. According to the author, why are some oil companies in
   favor of ratifying the Law of the Sea Treaty (LOST)?

Ben Lerner, "LOST Oil Prophets," *American Spectator*, July 14, 2008. Copyright © The American Spectator 2008. Reproduced by permission.

2. According to the American Petroleum Institute (API) and other industry players, by how many square miles can the United States expand its mineral exploration/development area under LOST?

3. What is "the precautionary principle," according to the author?

Against the alarming backdrop of gasoline prices at over $4 a gallon, oil industry executives are busily working the halls of Congress to make the case for increasing domestic oil supply. In addition to pushing for access to the Arctic National Wildlife Refuge (ANWR) and oil reserves off the East and West coasts, however, some industry reps are also rehashing the argument that the Law of the Sea Treaty (LOST) [also known as Law of the Sea Convention] presents an opportunity further to secure American oil by "locking in" drilling rights in our Arctic continental shelf.

LOST Has Hidden Costs

It should arguably be self-evident to the oil industry, based upon its own long and difficult experience with trying to open up additional domestic sources, that LOST enthusiasts are promising much more than our politicians have shown a willingness to deliver. Were the industry to think things through and conduct its due diligence on this treaty, it would also be self-evident that LOST will impose severe costs on American oil companies, leaving the consumer stranded at the pump with even higher gasoline prices, after having been led to believe that salvation lies beneath the polar ice.

On paper, LOST provides a mechanism through which a state party can seek to expand the outer limits of its continental shelf beyond the standard 200 miles from shore, and exploit the natural resources within that area. Under procedures laid out in Annex II of the treaty, the petitioning party submits geologic data and makes its case for expansion before a

LOST body called the Commission on the Limits of the Continental Shelf, which then makes its determination as to the claim. The American Petroleum Institute [API] and other industry players have therefore estimated that under LOST, the U.S. could expand its mineral exploration/development area by just under 300,000 square miles.

Sounds like a great way to bring more oil online, and bring gasoline prices down, until one is faced with two harsh realities: the persistent division within Congress on domestic oil exploration, and the persistent agenda of the international community to "level" the global economic playing field at the expense of American enterprise.

Politics over New Oil Exploration

It has become abundantly clear over successive Congresses and administrations that the political will to expand domestic oil/gas extraction simply does not exist. Even now, with President [George W.] Bush pushing Congress to lift the ban on offshore exploration and open ANWR, Speaker [Nancy] Pelosi's response has been to dismiss these proposals as "more of the same failed policies of the past . . ."

This gridlock over ANWR and offshore drilling, of course, has been with us for decades. In 2005, even with a supportive president and a House and Senate controlled by largely supportive Republicans, ANWR leasing could not find its way into that year's energy bill. Merely considering the idea became a non-starter with the 2006 Democratic takeover of both chambers redefining the legislative landscape.

Offshore drilling has so far not fared any better. Repeated attempts to lift decades-old bans on it have failed, even with mechanisms thrown into energy legislation over the years that would have allowed coastal states the opportunity to permit or deny exploration at various distances off their respective coasts.

Environmentalists Use LOST Against Oil Companies

In a great ironic twist, the Law of the Sea Treaty [LOST]—supported by many in the energy sector—may give environmentalists a blunt instrument to use against the energy industry.

Article 212 of the treaty states, in part, "States shall adopt laws and regulations to prevent, reduce and control pollution of the marine environment from or through the atmosphere. . . . States, acting especially through competent international organizations . . . shall endeavor to establish global and regional rules, standards and recommended practices and procedures to prevent, reduce and control pollution." This sounds like a directive to impose Kyoto Protocol–style regulations designed to reduce state emissions of greenhouse gases. . . .

Backdoor implementation of the Kyoto Protocol might be advanced by arguing that U.S.'s anthropogenic greenhouse gas emissions (one-quarter of such emissions worldwide) are warming the planet, causing irreparable harm to coral reefs, home to the world's most biologically-diverse marine ecosystems.

Alternatively, they could argue that sea levels are rising due to U.S.-induced climate change, causing beach erosion in such countries as the Maldives, Comoros or the Seychelles. To bolster their case, they might cite Article 194(2) of the treaty which states: "States shall take all measures necessary to ensure that activities under their jurisdiction or control are so conducted as not to cause damage by pollution to other states and their environment."

David A. Ridenour, "Ratification of the Law of the Sea Treaty: A Not-So Innocent Passage," National Policy Analysis, *August 2006.*

Then there's the polar bear, which Interior Secretary [Dirk] Kempthorne announced in May [2008] he was listing as a threatened species under the Endangered Species Act [ESA]. Although his office has asserted that the listing will still allow energy production in Alaska, members of Congress—including Rep. Edward Markey, chairman of the House Select Committee on Energy Independence and Global Warming—have expressed strong objections to any such notion. Do we really believe none of this will resurface if oil companies are given the green light to drill in our section of the Arctic continental shelf?

No Real Benefits for U.S. Oil Companies

Given all of this, is there really any basis on which the oil industry can assume that more area on which to drill in theory will result in more drilling opportunities in practice? In all likelihood, any newly acquired continental shelf will likely be locked away with the rest of the oil prospects. As hopeful as the industry may be, pushing LOST to increase oil supply is ultimately akin to [the mythological] Sisyphus rolling his rock up the hill, doomed to watch it fall to the bottom yet again.

Suspending disbelief for the moment and assuming new drilling would be allowed, joining this treaty would be far from cost-free, either for the oil industry or for the American consumer. As has been thoroughly documented by Lawrence Kogan of the Institute for Trade, Standards and Sustainable Development [ITSSD], the marine environmental protection requirements emanating from LOST are rooted in the European-derived "precautionary principle," a legal tenet requiring assurance that a proposed action will cause *no harm* to the environment *before* proceeding. The costs of this regime are real, and the risk is not hyperbole—according to a recent front-page article from the *Washington Post*, American chemical companies must now conform to recently passed EU [European Union] laws premised exactly upon this principle, which affected companies are saying will add *billions* to their costs.

Other Pitfalls of LOST

Other pitfalls for the industry lie buried deep within the treaty text. LOST contains numerous technology transfer requirements that will undoubtedly be used to compel American oil companies to hand over sensitive technologies to other nations. LOST's provisions on prevention of marine pollution from land-based sources could easily serve as a convenient peg on which to hang the greenhouse gas–regulating Kyoto Protocol, even though that treaty has also never been ratified. All of these increased costs of doing business will predictably be passed on to the consumer, the addition of American Arctic oil to the market notwithstanding.

The American people are rightfully demanding solutions to our energy crisis, but make no mistake: LOST is not one of them. Big Oil's arguments to the contrary ignore the political track record on increasing domestic supply while underestimating the harm that LOST will likely inflict upon the industry, with the effect of *raising* gas prices, not lowering them. So much for locking in relief.

> "Our position is simply stated—The development of offshore renewable and traditional energy must be part of a comprehensive plan in which the states are full partners, addresses regional needs and opportunities and uses the best science possible."

U.S. Government Should Create a Comprehensive Energy Policy

Ted Diers

Ted Diers is the chairman of the Coastal States Organization (CSO). In the following testimony in front of the Committee on Natural Resources, he underscores the need for a comprehensive energy plan that includes the input of the coastal states and territories on offshore drilling to maintain state sovereignty in most areas and federal consistency in others.

As you read, consider the following questions:

1. How many states, commonwealths, and territories make up the Coastal States Organization (CSO)?

Ted Diers, "Offshore Drilling: State Perspectives," Congresssional Testimony: Oversight Hearing before the Committee on Natural Resources, February 24, 2009. Reproduced by permission of the author.

2. What does section 307 of the Coastal Zone Management Act (CZMA) dictate about the subject of state sovereignty?

3. What three things does Ted Diers feel should be included in a comprehensive energy plan?

Good morning, Mr. Chairman [Congressman Nick J. Rahall] and members of the committee. My name is Ted Diers and I am the manager of the New Hampshire Coastal Program of the New Hampshire Department of Environmental Services. I also serve as chair of the Coastal States Organization [CSO] which represents the governors of the nation's thirty-five coastal states on the sustainable management of the nation's oceans, Great Lakes and coastal resources. Thank you for holding this important hearing this afternoon and for inviting me to testify on behalf of the coastal states.

Let me start by saying that the thirty-five coastal states, territories, and commonwealths that are members of the Coastal States Organization are at the forefront of ocean and coastal management in this nation. Whether it's addressing sea level rise and hazards in the Gulf states, renewable energy proposals off the Northeast Coast, or coral bleaching in the Pacific Islands, coastal states are on the front lines of these issues. Our ocean and coastal resources are not only important to us at the state level, but to citizens throughout this nation.

Coastal and ocean areas also represent an important source of energy for the United States, including oil, natural gas, and renewable energy in the form of tidal, wave and wind energy. Use of the oceans for energy production requires a commitment to responsible development that promotes protection of living marine resources, seafloor habitats, and coastal communities. Such development must proceed from an understanding that our oceans are held in public trust for all citizens, and that multiple uses (including energy production) must be consistent with the long-term productivity of these resources.

Formulating a National Energy Policy

As the United States crafts a national energy policy, including coastal and offshore energy development, it is important to consider three key factors which I will address today: 1. the retention of state sovereignty and consistency authority; 2. the planning for the nation's Exclusive Economic Zone [EEZ] including traditional and renewable energy development; and 3. the establishment of a permanent trust fund.

Our position is simply stated—The development of offshore renewable and traditional energy must be part of a comprehensive plan in which the states are full partners, addresses regional needs and opportunities and uses the best science possible. And, that effective planning and good science has costs associated with it.

State Sovereignty and Consistency Authority

While offshore energy production benefits the entire nation, the impacts from activities associated with exploration, development and production on state coastal lands and federal offshore lands are felt most in coastal states. Thus, it is vital for state authority and sovereignty to be maintained. CSO recommends that Congress and the administration consult with coastal states in the development of any new leasing program or formula of revenue sharing. In the past, offshore moratoria have been the result of a fractured, exclusive and federally driven energy policy. If indeed we are heading in direction of a "post-moratorium" world, the ability for a state to review actions related to offshore oil and gas drilling is essential.

Section 307 of the Coastal Zone Management Act [CZMA], known as the federal consistency provision, grants states authority to review federal activities, licenses and permits that have reasonably foreseeable effects on any land or water use or natural resource of the coastal zone. These activities must be consistent to the maximum extent practicable with the enforceable policies of a coastal state's federally approved coastal management program. This has been a primary method of ensuring more sustainable development of the nation's coasts.

Consistency Is Imperative

Consistency applies before a federal permit is issued; thus, it facilitates early consultation between states, federal agencies and permit applicants in order to avert disputes from arising after substantial commitments have been made by agencies and applicants. In practice, consistency is important as a "ticket to the dance"—allowing states to have a seat at the table in decisions related to the coasts. Without these early reviews, there would be much more uncertainty, litigation and calls for federal legislative intervention in actions in coastal communities. To increase efficiency for states, federal agencies and applicants, many states have created streamlined approaches to energy-related activities.

In granting states consistency authority, Congress recognized that federal interests and activities must be balanced with the sovereign interests of states in managing coastal resources. This is the underlying philosophy of the CZMA and the consistency provision. State coastal programs must receive federal approval for a state to exercise its consistency authority; likewise, each enforceable policy upon which it relies must also receive federal approval.

Furthermore, the resources of the OCS and the coastal zone are many times difficult, if not impossible, to differentiate. Fish, currents, wind and waves care little about an imaginary line drawn three nautical miles from our shores. As the committee considers offshore energy, the retention of consistency under the CZMA must be a priority.

Renewable Energy Development

Given the prices and impacts of oil consumption, offshore oil and gas development must be considered in the context of the

Secretary of the Interior Ken Salazar on Comprehensive Energy Plan

"We need a new, comprehensive energy plan that takes us to the new energy frontier and secures our energy independence," [Ken] Salazar said. "We must embrace President [Barack] Obama's vision of energy independence for the sake of our national security, our economic security, and our environmental security."

Ken Salazar,
Department of Interior Press Release,
February 10, 2009.

development of renewable energy and both must be balanced with the care of oceans and coasts and the economic viability of coastal communities. The energy needs and even the offshore resources of any particular state do not occur in a vacuum. There is significant "regionality" to both offshore needs and opportunities. Thus, the regional scale is appropriate for science-based planning. The states are moving to take on some of these regional needs through the development of regional ocean partnerships. From the Gulf of Mexico Alliance to the West Coast Governors' Agreement [on Ocean Health], the Great Lakes Commission to my own backyard in the Northeast Regional Ocean Council, the states are working together to create the framework for large-scale problem solving. This regional ocean partnership movement is a distinct opportunity for the states and federal government to work together.

Development of diverse and numerous sources of alternative renewable energy is critical to our nation's energy security and environmental well-being. The federal role is crucial because virtually every site where ocean renewable energy technology is likely to be tested or deployed is subject to federal jurisdiction. Unlike conventional wind and solar, ocean renewable energy technology cannot be tested or deployed on private land. The industry will emerge and mature in the United States only if the federal government uses its resources and authorities to plan for and encourage appropriate use of the marine areas it controls.

While the Minerals Management Service [MMS] plans for offshore oil and gas drilling, no federal or interstate body has taken on the task of planning for renewable energy development. Furthermore, there are myriad other coastal offshore uses and resources to consider when planning for energy development. CSO encourages the consideration of renewable energy in a national energy policy and legislation, including planning that addresses uses, resources and impacts.

Establishment of a Permanent Trust Fund

Great science and planning cost money. In the first OCS hearing in this series by the committee on February 10 [2009], Chairman Rahall, you noted that "money from the ocean appears to go to everything but the ocean." Indeed, even though coastal states are affected exponentially by the impacts of offshore energy development, receipts derived from sales, bonus bids and royalties under the mineral leasing laws are paid to the treasury through the Minerals Management Service [MMS]. But, these revenues are not directly applied to pay for federal or state agencies' examination, monitoring and managing wildlife, fish, water and other natural resources related to energy and mineral exploration and development.

The establishment of a trust fund provides a mechanism for reinvestment of the revenues generated from these public lands toward protection of coastal resources and communities. The trust fund can support the focused efforts of coastal states, territories and commonwealths, other appropriate coastal authorities, and federal agencies in addressing critical ocean and coastal management needs of our nation including restoration, protection, and enhancement of natural processes and habitats. This will help minimize the impacts of relative sea level rise, global warming, and ocean acidification and provide technical assistance and research to better anticipate and plan for the impacts of global warming and ocean acidification on ocean and coastal resources.

Challenges Faced by U.S. Coastal Regions

In its final report, the U.S. Commission on Ocean Policy identified a myriad of challenges to improve the management of our nation's ocean and coastal resources. The commission recognized that to meet these challenges additional investments would be necessary, and Outer Continental Shelf [OCS] receipts were identified as the primary source of funding. Additionally, the commission recommended that a portion of OCS revenues should be shared with coastal states (Recommendation 24-1). Revenues shared with the states should further the goals of improved coastal and ocean management.

In 2006, the Coastal States Organization [CSO] adopted a policy on revenue sharing which states that "because the coastal states face a number of challenges in conserving their coastal resources and protecting their coastal communities, OCS receipts should be used to further the goals of coastal and ocean restoration, conservation, preservation, mitigation, research and education." While the coastal states may not agree on the presence of offshore oil and gas drilling off their shores, they do agree in the reinvestment of funds from these public resources. Furthermore, these funds should be provided over and above existing appropriations to meet the increasingly complex and unmet needs of ocean and coastal managers.

It has been said that we know more about the surface of Mars than we do about the bottom of the ocean. The problem with that is we are not yet trying to manage use conflicts on Mars, but we are here on Earth.

Legislation Considerations

The oceans will continue to play an important role in access to sustainable and reliable energy. By retaining the state review authority, reinvesting a portion of public trust revenues on marine and coastal resources, and planning for both traditional and renewable energy development, new energy legislation will enhance our nation's ability to meet pressing ocean and coastal needs in an economical, efficient and sustained manner.

In legislation regarding OCS activities, CSO requests:

- Federal consistency authority under the Coastal Zone Management Act should be maintained and states' authority within their own jurisdictions should not be weakened in any way.

- Congress and the administration should commit to planning for the EEZ that includes energy policy based on development of traditional and renewable energy sources, and is enhanced by state-led regional partnerships.

- Revenues should be shared with coastal states and used to further the goals of coastal and ocean management, restoration, conservation, preservation, mitigation and research.

Thank you again for the opportunity to address the committee and for holding this important series of hearings. The Coastal States Organization stands ready to work with you to continue this progress of making important improvements to energy policy and coastal and ocean management. We look forward to the advancements that we can make in the coming year.

> "[Opening up new regions for offshore drilling] is not the entire answer to the energy challenge we face, by any means, but the U.S. can't fashion an answer to its energy challenge without it."

Any U.S. Energy Policy Should Emphasize Offshore Drilling

Lamar McKay

Lamar McKay is the chairman and chief executive officer (CEO) of BP America. In the following testimony before the Committee on Natural Resources, he argues that to meet America's growing energy challenges, we must develop every resource we have, including alternative energy sources such as biofuel, solar, and others. McKay states that opening up new offshore areas for drilling must be part of that plan if America is to stay globally competitive.

As you read, consider the following questions:

1. According to Lamar McKay, how much money is BP America investing in biofuel research?

Lamar McKay, "Offshore Drilling: Industrial Perspectives," Congressional Testimony: Oversight Hearing before the Committee on Natural Resources, February 25, 2009.

2. The U.S. Department of the Interior (DOI) estimates that how many gallons of fuel may lie in unexplored areas of the Outer Continental Shelf (OCS)?

3. What does BP's track record in the Gulf of Mexico show about offshore drilling?

BP appreciates the opportunity to appear before this panel and present our views on exploring for potential new sources of oil and natural gas in areas of the federal Outer Continental Shelf (OCS). The needs of our country require that we explore for new domestic sources of energy that are secure and reliable in good times and in tough times.

I represent the 33,000 employees at BP working in the United States. We are not only the largest oil and gas producer in the United States, but also the company that invests in the most diverse energy portfolio in the industry. Since 2004, we have invested more than $34 billion in the United States to increase existing energy sources, extend energy supplies and develop new low-carbon technologies.

BP's investments stretch from the Gulf of Mexico to the North Slope of Alaska and from the East Coast to the Midwest and the West Coast. Our over 13,000 service stations—most of them locally owned and operated—are a familiar part of the American landscape.

The company's major spending programs also touch every major segment of the energy industry, from exploration and production of oil and natural gas through refining and distribution of fuel products, as well as renewables.

BP Invests in Diverse Energy Sources

By heavily investing in a diverse range of energy sources—from traditional oil and natural gas production to renewable energy including biofuels, solar, wind and hydrogen power—BP is helping meet America's energy needs today while moving towards a more secure energy future.

In 2008, BP's U.S. production of liquid hydrocarbons was 538,000 bpd [barrels per day] about 10 percent of U.S. domestic production and the largest of any single producer. Our gas production was over 2 bcfd [billion cubic feet per day].

BP's solar business has been in operation for over 30 years and last year had sales of 162 MW [megawatts] globally. This represents an increase of 29% over 2007 and expectations are there will be significant growth through 2009.

We are major investors in wind generation and have amassed a land portfolio capable of potentially supporting up to 20,000 megawatts (MW) of wind generation, one of the largest positions in the country. As of year-end 2008, BP and its partners had 1,000 MW of wind generation online and expect to have an installed capacity of approximately 2,000 MW of wind power by the end of 2010.

We are one of the largest blenders and marketers of biofuels in the nation. Last year, BP blended over 1 billion gallons of ethanol with gasoline. We are underwriting cutting-edge research—investing more than $500 million over the next 10 years—in the search for a new generation of biofuels. We believe these will contain more energy, have less impact on the environment, and will not reduce the supply or increase the cost of food.

BP Supports Comprehensive Approach to Problem

Overall, we support an energy policy that promotes the development of both traditional and nontraditional sources of energy, as well as conservation and efficiency. At the same time, our approach has been shaped by some stark realities about America's energy outlook.

Stark Realities

The relatively low oil and gasoline prices American consumers are now enjoying masks the fact that our country faces tremendous energy challenges. Years of contradictory public policies, poor market dynamics and company decisions have combined to limit access to resources, discourage development and constrain new investment. No company or industry on its own is large enough or powerful enough to change the conditions that brought us here. But energy companies, policy makers and consumers together have roles to play in creating a new energy future for our country.

This relationship must be shaped by the recognition that the U.S. economy needs both to better conserve energy and to produce more energy of every type to meet future growth. We need to invest in conventional oil and gas. We also need to invest in renewables to begin the transition to a lower-carbon future. However, we must all understand that this future is many years away and that these new energy sources will not make a large contribution to total U.S. energy supply for many years.

2007 Study on Truths About Energy

This view is reflected in a 2007 study issued by the National Petroleum Council—*Facing the Hard Truths About Energy*. I have integrated its observations and conclusions below and added emphasis as necessary:

> There is no single, easy solution to the global challenges ahead. Given the massive scale of the global energy system and the long lead times necessary to make material changes, actions must be initiated now and sustained over the long term. Over the next 25 years, the United States and the world face hard truths about the global energy future:
>
> - Coal, oil, and natural gas will remain indispensable to meeting total projected energy demand growth.
>
> - The world is not running out of energy resources, but there are accumulating risks to continuing expansion of oil and natural gas production from the conventional

sources relied upon historically. These risks create significant challenges to meeting projected total energy demand.

- To mitigate these risks, expansion of all economic energy sources will be required, including coal, nuclear, biomass, other renewables, and unconventional oil and natural gas. Each of these sources faces significant challenges including safety, environmental, political, or economic hurdles, and imposes infrastructure requirements for development and delivery.

Era of Big Oil Is Done

The benign energy environment we are now experiencing may not last. Growth in the demand for energy will resume when our economy starts growing again. The U.S. Energy Information Administration (EIA) projects that energy demand will increase 11 percent by 2030. If anticipated U.S. needs are combined with those of the rest of the world, at growth rates of 3 percent, EIA projects that a 35 percent expansion in global oil production will be needed. That equates to an additional 30 million barrels of oil every day.

Finding that oil will be neither simple nor cheap. The era of "easy oil" may be over. New supplies are harder to find, more difficult and more expensive to extract, and are often located in politically unstable parts of the world. Wherever they come from, bringing new supplies to fuel our homes, businesses and transportation needs will require the investment of hundreds of billions of dollars.

There Is Oil in America

Let me take the opportunity to put to rest a major energy myth, namely that there is no more energy to be found here in the U.S.

In fact, the United States is a sleeping giant when it comes to energy.

- We have a 100-year supply of coal. There is little doubt that with "clean coal" and carbon capture technology, we could be using a lot more coal in the coming decades to heat our homes and recharge our electric cars.

- We have huge deposits of oil shale in many of our western states.

- We have the potential to generate much more safe, clean, reliable electricity via nuclear energy than we are doing today.

But until technologies such as clean coal, carbon capture and renewable sources can come online in a major way, far and away the greatest potential source of new domestic energy supply is the oil and natural gas that lies off our shores.

U.S. Shoots Itself in the Foot

Here in the U.S., we have deliberately constrained our own supply by limiting access to promising areas for leasing, exploration and development. American domestic oil production has fallen by around 4 million barrels per day since 1985. At the same time, demand has risen by roughly similar amounts, so the gap must be filled by imports.

And when world demand rises—as it did recently, particularly in China and India—it makes those imports more expensive. That accounts in part for the dramatic rise in oil prices we experienced last summer [2008].

A more secure and reliable source of energy closer to home is also essential to our country's long-term economic and energy well-being. As we have seen repeatedly since the first oil shock in 1973, wildly spiking and plunging oil prices kill jobs. Energy drives economic growth but few businesses—as we are seeing now—are willing to make investments in an atmosphere of great uncertainty.

Limiting U.S. Oil Production Risks Our Economy

The slowing of investment—the number of operating U.S. oil rigs has fallen to 1399, the lowest number since July 2005—presents a real risk to our economy. Prices could rise once again when the recovery occurs because investment may not be sufficient to offset the natural decline in the resource base. The challenge for all of us is to not allow this cyclical decline to create a structural loss in capacity. We must continue to invest in new technology and infrastructure development at the bottom of the cycle to provide continued access to supplies.

Areas of the OCS that have historically been off-limits to exploration can and should play a substantial role in closing this supply gap as well as securing our economic future. It is not the entire answer to the energy challenge we face, by any means, but the U.S. can't fashion an answer to its energy challenge without it.

A Department of the Interior [DOI] study estimates the amount of oil to be found in areas that have been off-limits to exploration at 17.8 billion barrels. That's equal to 30 years of U.S. imports from Saudi Arabia. The same study put natural gas reserves at 76 trillion cubic feet, or enough to meet America's requirements for over 10 years.

These are DOI estimates. There could be more. There could also be less. We can't know unless we are given the opportunity to lease and explore.

Offshore Oil Development Is a Long and Expensive Process

The journey from access to production is a long one. A tremendous amount of preparation as well as infrastructure, both onshore and offshore, is required for successful development.

That's why we support a thoughtful and deliberate approach to this issue. As a first step, we propose the acquisition

Karen A. Harbert on a Comprehensive Energy Policy

But those who would say we can attain energy security without oil or natural gas are as incorrect as those who would say that we can drill our way out of our current energy challenges. The only way we can effectively meet our energy demands is with an approach that includes a myriad of resources, including oil, gas and renewables. Just as we can't ignore the promise of renewable energy, we also cannot ignore the reality of our continued need for oil and natural gas.

Karen A. Harbert, "Offshore Drilling: Industrial Perspectives," Oversight Hearing before the Committee of Natural Resources, February 25, 2009.

of new regional 2-D seismic data in the OCS in order to identify the most prospective regions. From there, closely spaced 2-D or 3-D seismic data can be acquired to identify the best prospects in each area. Such surveys are costly and complex to plan and implement, but vastly increase the information content. This "virtual drilling" protects the environment by providing greater accuracy in mapping deposits and reduces the need for drilling exploratory wells.

BP in the Gulf of Mexico

The track record of BP and the industry generally in the Western and Central Gulf of Mexico (GOM) demonstrates that when areas are opened, they can be leased, explored and developed to the highest environmental and operational standards in the world.

Our investments in the Gulf of Mexico are a remarkable American success story. Since 1985, oil production from the deepwater gulf has increased 15-fold, from 58,000 to 870,000 barrels per day, or more than one in six barrels of oil produced in the United States. It's also more than all the oil the United States imported on an average day from Angola, Indonesia, Kuwait, Libya, and Russia combined in 2007.

We operate in water depths that exceed 1 1/2 miles—more than six Empire State Buildings stacked one on top of another—and well depths as great as 30,000 feet—the normal cruising altitude of a commercial passenger jet.

Further, we have had to cope with operating temperatures and pressures greater than any we have ever experienced. For example, a typical military fighter jet is capable of operating in an 8 G environment, while oil and gas drilling tools regularly experience forces in excess of 200 Gs. Despite these challenges, industry responded to government encouragement to invest, explore and develop the deepwater resource base.

The dramatic rise in deep water production in the GOM also demonstrates an elemental truth about our business: The more we know, the more we can produce. As knowledge and technology advance, deposits once thought to be beyond reach or uneconomical to extract eventually become viable.

Periodical Bibliography

The following articles have been selected to supplement the diverse views presented in this chapter.

David Freddoso — "Dems over a Domestic Barrel," *National Review Online*, July 30, 2008. www.national review.com.

Daniel Gross — "The Case (Almost) for Drilling," *Slate*, June 18, 2008.

Phil Kerpen — "Drilling for Victory," *National Review Online*, August 5, 2008. www.nationalreview.com.

Michael Klare — "Brace Yourselves for Life After Oil," Salon .com, September 24, 2009. www.salon.com.

Larry Kudlow — "An America First Energy Plan," *National Review Online*, July 2, 2008. www.national review.com.

Eric Peters — "Obama Nails the Coffin Shut," *American Spectator*, May 20, 2009.

Catharine Skipp and Arian Campo-Flores — "An Oily Mess," *Newsweek*, June 19, 2008. www.newsweek.com.

Daniel Stone — "Will Congress Finally Pass an Energy Bill?" *Newsweek*, September 15, 2008. www.news week.com.

Lee Hudson Teslik — "Who Owns the Arctic?" *Slate*, October 24, 2007.

Jon Basil Utley — "Open ANWR Already!" *Reason*, August 14, 2008.

For Further Discussion

Chapter 1

1. After reading the viewpoints by the Natural Resources Defense Council (NRDC) and Humberto Fontova, do you think that offshore drilling is environmentally responsible? Use the viewpoints to provide evidence to support your opinion.

2. William F. Jasper maintains that offshore drilling will be beneficial for the American economy by creating jobs and making gas prices more affordable and stable. Carolyn McCormick argues that it will hurt the economy, especially the fishing and tourism industries. Which viewpoint do you feel is more relevant and pressing in light of America's current economic problems?

3. In the past several years, the link between oil and national security has become a key U.S. concern. In his viewpoint, Andrew A. Michta argues that offshore drilling will strengthen U.S. national security. Michael T. Klare, however, counters by asserting that conservation and developing alternative and renewable fuel sources are better ways to protect American security. Whose viewpoint do you support, and why?

4. The use of biofuels is a hot issue in the debate over America's energy future. In his viewpoint, Chris Dannen outlines the advantages of biofuels compared to offshore drilling. Alan Caruba argues the opposite in his viewpoint. In light of the information provided by both authors, where do you stand in the biofuels versus offshore drilling debate?

Chapter 2

1. Energy independence is a goal that many energy experts discuss. Arthur B. Laffer contends that offshore drilling will eventually decrease our dependence on foreign oil imports. Paul Craig Roberts scoffs at that view, arguing that offshore drilling will not make a discernible difference in America's dependence on foreign oil. In your view, where does the truth lie? How can America decrease its energy dependence?

2. Kevin A. Hassett maintains that offshore drilling will significantly lower oil prices. Bryan K. Mignone argues that any price drop will be insignificant—and definitely not worth the other costs associated with offshore drilling. With whom do you concur, and why?

3. Should a moratorium on offshore drilling be considered an assault on the American middle class? That is what Peter Ferrara contends in his viewpoint. Do you find this argument persuasive, or do you agree with Tyson Slocum, who views offshore drilling as a way to enrich oil companies and hurt the middle class?

4. Environmental concerns are central to any discussion of offshore drilling. Do you agree with Andrew Leonard, who articulates his belief that offshore drilling will accelerate global warming, or with Alan Caruba, who argues that it will not? Which elements of the argument persuaded you?

Chapter 3

1. Drilling off the coast of Alaska has generated a heated debate. After reading the viewpoints of Marvin E. Odum and Margaret Williams, do you believe we should limit or expand Alaskan offshore drilling? Explain your answer.

2. What are "use it or lose it" laws and do you believe that they should be expanded or eliminated? Read the viewpoints of Russ Feingold and Newt Gingrich with Roy Innis to help with your answer.

Chapter 4

1. Do you believe that fuel efficiency standards should be raised? Read the viewpoints by Ian Parry and Jerry Taylor with Peter Van Doren to help formulate your opinion.

2. David B. Sandalow asserts that the Law of the Sea Treaty (LOST) should be ratified. In his viewpoint, Ben Lerner argues that it should not. After reading about LOST in both viewpoints, do you think that LOST should be ratified? Why or why not?

3. Many energy experts argue that the United States needs a comprehensive energy policy to meet its energy needs. In his viewpoint, Ted Diers makes this very point. Lamar McKay, however, counters that any U.S. energy policy must hold a prominent place for offshore drilling, which he asserts is key to any energy discussion. What do you see as the place of offshore drilling in a comprehensive energy policy? How important is offshore drilling to America's energy future?

Organizations to Contact

The editors have compiled the following list of organizations concerned with the issues debated in this book. The descriptions are derived from materials provided by the organizations. All have publications or information available for interested readers. The list was compiled on the date of publication of the present volume; the information provided here may change. Be aware that many organizations take several weeks or longer to respond to inquiries, so allow as much time as possible.

American Gas Association (AGA)

400 North Capitol Street NW, Suite 450
Washington, DC   20001
(202) 824-7000
Web site: www.aga.org

American Gas Association (AGA), founded in 1918, represents 202 local energy companies that deliver natural gas throughout the United States. AGA is an advocate for natural gas utility companies and their customers and provides a broad range of programs and services for natural gas pipeline members, marketers, gatherers, international natural gas companies, and industry associates. AGA also provides information and services that promote the safe and efficient delivery of natural gas—including the exploration for and drilling and transportation of natural gas. It offers a plethora of information on the natural gas industry, including the monthly *American Gas* magazine, which publishes articles on natural gas issues.

Americans for Prosperity (AFP)

2111 Wilson Boulevard, Suite 350, Arlington, VA   22201
(866) 730-0150
e-mail: info@AFPhq.org
Web site: www.americansforprosperity.org

Americans for Prosperity (AFP) is a conservative advocacy group that aims to educate citizens about economic policy and urges them to become active in the public policy process. AFP promotes policies that support limited government and champions the principles of entrepreneurship, free markets, and fiscal and regulatory restraint. Its educational programs and analyses promote the American enterprise system as the best way to ensure prosperity for all Americans. The AFP Web site contains news and information on offshore drilling and other energy issues, a blog, and a regional breakdown of events.

Consumer Watchdog
1750 Ocean Park Boulevard, Suite 200
Santa Monica, CA   90405
(310) 392-0522 • fax: (310) 392-8874
e-mail: admin@consumerwatchdog.org
Web site: www.consumerwatchdog.org

Consumer Watchdog is a national consumer advocacy group that works to save Americans billions of dollars and improve lives by fighting for the interests of patients, ratepayers, and policyholders. It lobbies for laws and regulations that prevent corporations and politicians from taking advantage of the American public and endangering lives and the environment. One of its major projects is Oil Watchdog, a blog and resource library about energy issues. Oil Watchdog investigates the links between oil companies and the media, especially so-called "independent" spokespeople funded by oil company money, and the lobbying activities of the big oil companies in Congress. It also hosts information on offshore drilling, the industry's fight against clean energy, and the hold big oil companies have on U.S. energy policy.

Energy Future Coalition
1800 Massachusetts Avenue NW, 4th Floor
Washington, DC   20036
(202) 463-1947

e-mail: info@energyfuturecoalition.org
Web site: www.energyfuturecoalition.org

Energy Future Coalition is a nonpartisan public policy initiative that promotes and facilitates the transition to a new energy economy. The coalition brings business, labor, and environmental groups together to identify new directions in energy policy with broad political support. It also works closely with the United Nations Foundation on energy and climate policy, especially energy efficiency and bioenergy issues. Energy Future Coalition publishes reports and articles about America's dependence on fossil fuels and the process of transitioning to alternative energy sources. It also provides information on green jobs and opportunities.

Independent Petroleum Association of America (IPAA)

1201 Fifteenth Street NW, Suite 300, Washington, DC 20005
(202) 857-4722 • fax: (202) 857-4799
e-mail: Webmaster@ipaa.org
Web site: www.ipaa.org

Independent Petroleum Association of America (IPAA) is a national trade association representing independent oil and natural gas producers and service companies, who develop 90 percent of domestic oil and gas wells, 68 percent of domestic oil, and 82 percent of domestic natural gas. IPAA advocates and lobbies for the interests of its members with the U.S. Congress, federal agencies, and the administration. It also researches and provides economic and statistical information about the exploration and development of offshore wells. The IPAA publishes a weekly newsletter, *Washington Report*, which covers legislative and regulatory issues within the industry. The IPAA Web site also provides reports and statistical studies covering the oil and gas industries and supply and demand forecasts.

Institute for Energy Research (IER)

1100 H Street NW, Suite 400, Washington, DC 20005
(202) 621-2950 • fax: (202) 637-2420

Web site: www.instituteforenergyresearch.org

Founded in 1989, the Institute for Energy Research (IER) is a not-for-profit organization that conducts research and analysis on the functions, operations, and government regulation of global energy markets. IER promotes the idea that unfettered energy markets provide the most efficient and effective solutions to today's global energy and environmental challenges and works to educate legislators, policy makers, and the public of the vital role offshore drilling plays in America's energy future. It publishes fact sheets and comprehensive studies on renewable and nonrenewable energy sources, the growing green economy, climate change, and offshore oil exploration and drilling opportunities. IER also maintains a blog on its Web site, which provides timely comments on relevant energy and legislative issues.

Natural Resources Defense Council (NRDC)

40 West Twentieth Street, New York, NY 10011
(212) 727-2700 • fax: (212) 727-1773
e-mail: nrdcinfo@nrdc.org
Web site: www.nrdc.org

Founded in 1970, Natural Resources Defense Council (NRDC) is an advocate for U.S. wildlife and the environment. It has played an integral role in writing and passing some of America's most stringent environmental legislation, and it actively lobbies the U.S. government to pass laws and regulations that will preserve America's wild areas, oceans, and indigenous animals. NRDC works to find and implement solutions to the world's most pressing environmental issues, such as alleviating global warming, transitioning from oil and fossil fuels to alternative sources of energy, protecting the oceans, and improving China's environmental record. The NRDC Web site provides information on environmental issues, including fact sheets, position papers, and reports, and offers opportunities to get involved in environmental activism.

Sierra Club
85 Second Street, 2nd Floor, San Francisco, CA 94105
(415) 977-5500 • fax: (415) 977-5799
e-mail: information@sierraclub.org
Web site: www.sierraclub.org

Sierra Club is the oldest and largest grassroots environmental organization in the United States. It works to ensure safe and healthy communities; implement smart energy solutions to combat global warming; and create an enduring legacy for America's wildlife and natural environment. Sierra Club publishes *Sierra* magazine, blogs on the environment and Sierra Club activities, and e-mail newsletters, mostly geared toward students. The organization's major concern is the environmental impact of offshore exploration and drilling. It provides information on the latest developments and opportunities for people to get involved in the fight against offshore drilling.

Society of Petroleum Engineers (SPE)
222 Palisades Creek Drive, Richardson, TX 75080-2040
(972) 952-9393 • fax: (972) 952-9435
e-mail: spedal@spe.org
Web site: www.spe.org

Society of Petroleum Engineers (SPE) is an international professional organization for petroleum engineers devoted to collecting, disseminating, and exchanging technical knowledge about the exploration, development, and production of oil and gas resources. SPE supports the development of more efficient and environmentally sound technologies for the public benefit. SPE publishes scholarly books and reports and the monthly *Journal of Petroleum Technology*, which presents authoritative briefs and features on exploration and production technology, oil industry and gas industry issues, and news about SPE and its members.

Union of Concerned Scientists (UCS)
2 Brattle Square, Cambridge, MA 02238-9105
(617) 547-5552 • fax: (617) 864-9405

Web site: www.ucsusa.org

Founded by scientists and students at the Massachusetts Institute of Technology (MIT) in 1969, the Union of Concerned Scientists (UCS) is the leading science-based nonprofit group working toward a healthy environment and a safer world. UCS utilizes independent scientific research and citizen action "to develop innovative practical solutions and to secure responsible changes in government policy, corporate practices, and consumer choices." UCS publishes reports on important issues such as global warming, scientific integrity, clean energy and vehicles, global security, and food and agriculture. It also publishes *Catalyst* magazine, *Earthwise* newsletter, and *Greentips* e-newsletter.

U.S. Department of Energy (DOE)
1000 Independence Avenue SW, Washington, DC   20585
(202) 586-5000 • fax: (202) 586-4403
e-mail: The.Secretary@hq.doe.gov
Web site: www.energy.gov

The U.S. Department of Energy (DOE) is a government department tasked with advancing the national, economic, and energy security of the United States. The DOE also promotes scientific and technological innovation in support of energy security and crafts legislation aimed to make the United States more energy efficient and independent. The DOE is active in the debate surrounding offshore oil and natural gas exploration and development, and provides news and information on its Web site. The DOE advocates for the development of clean energy sources including wind, solar energy, hydropower, and geothermal energy. E-mail updates and e-newsletters are available.

U.S. Energy Association (USEA)
1300 Pennsylvania Avenue NW, Suite 550, Mailbox 142
Washington, DC   20004-3022
(202) 312-1230 • fax: (202) 682-1682
e-mail: reply@usea.org

Web site: www.usea.org

The United States Energy Association (USEA), the U.S. member of the World Energy Council, is an association of public and private energy-related organizations, corporations, and government agencies that promotes the interests of the U.S. energy sector by increasing the understanding of energy issues. USEA supports the mission of the World Energy Council "to promote the sustainable supply and use of energy for the greatest benefit of all." In conjunction with the U.S. Agency for International Development (USAID) and the U.S. Department of Energy (DOE), USEA sponsors the Energy Partnership Program. It also sponsors and publishes policy reports and conferences about global and domestic energy issues.

Bibliography of Books

John Scales Avery   *Energy, Resources, and the Long-Term Future*. Hackensack, NJ: World Scientific, 2007.

Gawdat Bahgat   *American Oil Diplomacy in the Persian Gulf and the Caspian Sea*. Gainesville, FL: University Press of Florida, 2003.

Carolyn Barta   *ENSCO: The First Twenty Years: Offshore Driller of Choice*. Houston, TX: Gulf Publications, 2008.

Jerome R. Corsi and Craig R. Smith   *Black Gold Stranglehold: The Myth of Scarcity and the Politics of Oil*. Nashville, TN: WND Books, 2005.

John S. Duffield   *Over a Barrel: The Costs of U.S. Foreign Oil Dependence*. Stanford, CA: Stanford Law and Politics, 2008.

Rebecca Harman   *The Earth's Resources*. Chicago: Heinemann, 2005.

Mike Heffernan   *Rig: An Oral History of the Ocean Ranger Disaster*. St. John's, Newfoundland, Canada: Creative Publishers, 2009.

Dieter Helm, ed.   *The New Energy Paradigm*. Oxford, UK: Oxford University Press, 2007.

Dilip Hiro   *Blood of the Earth: The Battle for the World's Vanishing Oil Resources*. New York: Nation Books, 2007.

Thomas Homer-Dixon, ed.

Carbon Shift: How the Twin Crises of Oil Depletion and Climate Change Will Define the Future. Toronto: Random House Canada, 2009.

Philippe Le Billon, ed.

The Geopolitics of Resource Wars: Resource Dependence, Governance and Violence. London: Frank Cass, 2005.

Peter M. Lewis

Growing Apart: Oil, Politics, and Economic Change in Indonesia and Nigeria. Ann Arbor, MI: University of Michigan Press, 2007.

Daniel Moran and James A. Russell, eds.

Energy Security and Global Politics: The Militarization of Resource Management. New York: Routledge, 2008.

Craig Morris

Energy Switch: Proven Solutions for a Renewable Future. Gabriola Island, British Columbia, Canada: New Society Publishers, 2006.

Sheila Newman, ed.

The Final Energy Crisis. London: Pluto Press, 2008.

Peter R. Odell

Why Carbon Fuels Will Dominate the 21st Century's Global Energy Economy. Brentwood, England: Multi-Science Publications, 2004.

Chris Oxlade

How We Use Oil. Chicago: Raintree, 2004.

Francisco Parra

Oil Politics: A Modern History of Petroleum. New York: I.B. Tauris, 2004.

John T. Perry, ed.   *Energy Prices: Supply, Demand or Speculation?* Hauppauge, NY: Nova Science Publishers, 2009.

Dale Allen Pfeiffer   *Eating Fossil Fuels: Oil, Food and the Coming Crisis in Agriculture.* Gabriola Island, British Columbia, Canada: New Society Publishers, 2006.

Paul Roberts   *The End of Oil: On the Edge of a Perilous New World.* Boston: Houghton Mifflin, 2004.

Hope E. Robertson   *Focusing on the Demand Side of the Power Equation: Implications and Opportunities.* Cambridge, MA: CERA, 2006.

Julia Ruggeri   *Life Offshore.* Austin, TX: Petroleum Extension Service, University of Texas at Austin, 2007.

David Sandalow   *Freedom from Oil: How the Next President Can End the United States' Oil Addiction.* New York: McGraw-Hill, 2008.

Toby Shelley   *Oil: Politics, Poverty & the Planet.* New York: Zed Publishing, 2005.

Jill Sherman   *Oil and Energy Alternatives.* Edina, MN: ABDO Publishing, 2009.

Max Siollun   *Oil, Politics and Violence: Nigeria's Military Coup Culture.* New York: Algora, 2009.

Benjamin Smith   *Hard Times in the Lands of Plenty: Oil Politics in Iran and Indonesia.* Ithaca, NY: Cornell University Press, 2007.

John Tabak   *Coal and Oil.* New York: Facts On File, 2009.

Denise Walker   *Fuel and the Environment.* North Mankato, MN: Smart Apple Media, 2008.

Index

A

Abu Dhabi National Oil Company, 51
Afghanistan conflict, 2001-, 50, 55
Ahmadinejad, Mahmoud, 53
Alaska, *132*
   Arctic National Wildlife Refuge (ANWR), 39, 61, 69, 87, 93, 102, 116, 121, 128, 137, 191
   drilling should be expanded, 130–133
   drilling should be limited, 134–140
   oil capacity, production, and industry, 128–129, *132*
   oil spills, 23, 28, 30, 137–138, 140, 145
Alaska Marine Conservation Council, 132
Algae, as fuel source, 70, 72–74, 75
Alternative energy sources. *See* Renewable and alternative energy
Amoco Cadiz oil spill, 23
Animals. *See* Endangered animals; Marine life
Arctic areas
   environmental assessment, 142
   exploration support, 124, 190
   sensitivities/vulnerabilities, 129, 136, 138, 142–143
   See also Alaska; Arctic National Wildlife Refuge (ANWR)

Arctic National Wildlife Refuge (ANWR)
   drilling con- stance, 87, 116
   drilling consideration, 39, 61, 69, 87, 93, 102, 128, 191
   off-limits, 121, 137, 191
Argo Merchant oil spill, 23
Auto manufacturers, 163, 166, 169

B

Bahrain, 51
Bans, drilling. *See* Moratoria on drilling
Beach erosion, 192
Beaufort sea, Alaska, 135–136, 138
Big Oil. *See* Oil companies
Bingaman, Jeff, 152
Bioaccumulation, 31
Biofuels
   BP investment and development, 205
   future materials, 73, 74–75, 76
   less beneficial than drilling, 65–69
   more beneficial than drilling, 70–76
Boehner, John, 154
BP
   Alaskan oil spills, 138
   CEO opinions, energy policy, 203–211
   Gulf of Mexico exploration, 210–211
   Iraq operations, 56
   lawsuits, refinery pollution, 103

tourism jobs and revenues, 42, 43, 45–46

trust fund support, 200–201

See also Fishing industry; Tourism and recreation industries

Coastal States Organization (CSO), 195, 196–202

Coastal Zone Management Act (1972), 197–198, 202

Comprehensive Energy Policy Act (1992), 152

Congressional legislation and policy, 100

biofuels support, 65, 66–67

drilling halts, Outer Continental Shelf, 15, 33, 34–35, 38–40, 69, 132–133, 142, 145, 147–148

drilling reconsideration, Outer Continental Shelf, 35–38, 56, 79, 96, 105, 110–112, 145, 146–150, 203–211

environmental conservation and protection, 114, 121–122

fuel efficiency standards, 163–164, 165–170, 171–175

Law of the Sea Treaty (LOST) debate, 176–188, 189–194

"use it or lose it" laws, 151–156, 157–160

See also Energy policy, U.S.; House Committee on Natural Resources; Senate Committee on Foreign Relations

ConocoPhillips, 75

Conservation, need within energy policy, 59, 61, 63, 94, 118, 139, 142, 160, 206

See also Environmental movement

Conservation groups. *See* Environmental movement; Oceana; World Wildlife Fund (WWF)

Convention on the High Seas (1958), 181

Convention on the Law of the Sea. *See* Law of the Sea Treaty (LOST)

Coon, Charli E., 173

Coral reefs, 25–26, 143, 192, 196

Corn crops, and ethanol, 67, 71, 72

Corporate Average Fuel Economy (CAFE) standards, 163–164, 173

should be raised, 165–170

should not be raised, 107, 171–175

Crude oil prices. *See* Oil prices (per barrel)

Cuba, 22, 34, 102, 124

Currencies, values, 49, 88, 93, 105

D

Dams, 103

Dannen, Chris, 70–76

Danson, Ted, 29

Debt, U.S., 55

Deep Ocean Energy Resources Act of 2006, 2008 (DOER; bill), 35–38, 40, 110

Deep seabed mining, 178–179, 182–183, 186–188

Deep Water Royalty Relief Act (1995), 112

Demand for oil. *See* Supply and demand

Democratic Party

biofuels support, 65, 66–67

oil companies' opinions, 132–
133, 209
"post-moratorium" desires,
197
should be reinstated, 141–145
should not be reinstated, 146–
150
See also Outer Continental
Shelf
Muds, drilling, 31
Myers, Richard B., 180

N

National Academy of Sciences, oil
spill information, 30, 142–143
National Environmental Policy Act
(1969), 121
National Environmental Protection Act (1969), 114
National Highway Traffic Safety
Administration (NHTSA), 163
National Historic Preservation Act
(1966), 121
National Iranian Oil Company, 51,
53
National Petroleum Council, 206
National security
alternative fuel development
will strengthen, U.S., 58,
59–64
American policy, 20th century,
53–55
American policy, 21st century,
19–20, 61–63, 174, 199
fuel efficiency and, 167, 174
naval, 177, 179–182
offshore drilling will
strengthen, U.S., 22, 47–58,
66

Russian, 52
supply control and, 56, 58
Nationalized oil supplies, 55, 56
Norway, 115
Saudi Arabia, 50–51
Natural gas market, 57, 58
Natural oil seeps, 24, 25
Natural Resources Defense Coun-
cil
biofuels support, 73
data: oil spills, 143
data: value of tourism to
coastal states, 43
lawsuits, refineries, 103
opinion: drilling is environ-
mentally irresponsible, 27–32
opinion: efficient vehicles, 168
Navy, U.S., 179, 180–181, 188
Nigeria, 115
North Carolina's Outer Banks, 41,
42–46
North Korea, 174, 186
North Sea drilling, 115
North Slope oil fields, Alaska, 128,
138
Norway, 115
Nuclear ambitions (weapons), 62,
63, 174
Nuclear power, U.S., 57, 76, 84,
102–103, 208

O

Obama, Barack, 14
coal discouragement, 103
criticisms of American ex-
cesses, 108
drilling and nuclear discouragement, 83–84, 91, 118
election campaign, 2008, 86,
118, 124